HOUSE ON FIRE

WRITTEN, DRAWN, AND DESIGNED BY
MATT BATTAGLIA

EDITED BY
SEAN MICHAEL ROBINSON &
MICHAEL BATTAGLIA

DIGITAL PRODUCTION BY
SEAN MICHAEL ROBINSON

MARCH 2023. FIRST PRINTING

House on Fire © 2023 Matt Battaglia

First edition published 2023 by Living the Line LLC.

ISBN: 978-1-7368605-6-4

mattjbatt.com

livingthelinebooks.com

PRINTED IN CANADA by Marquis Imprimeur

FOR KALISTA AND HELEN

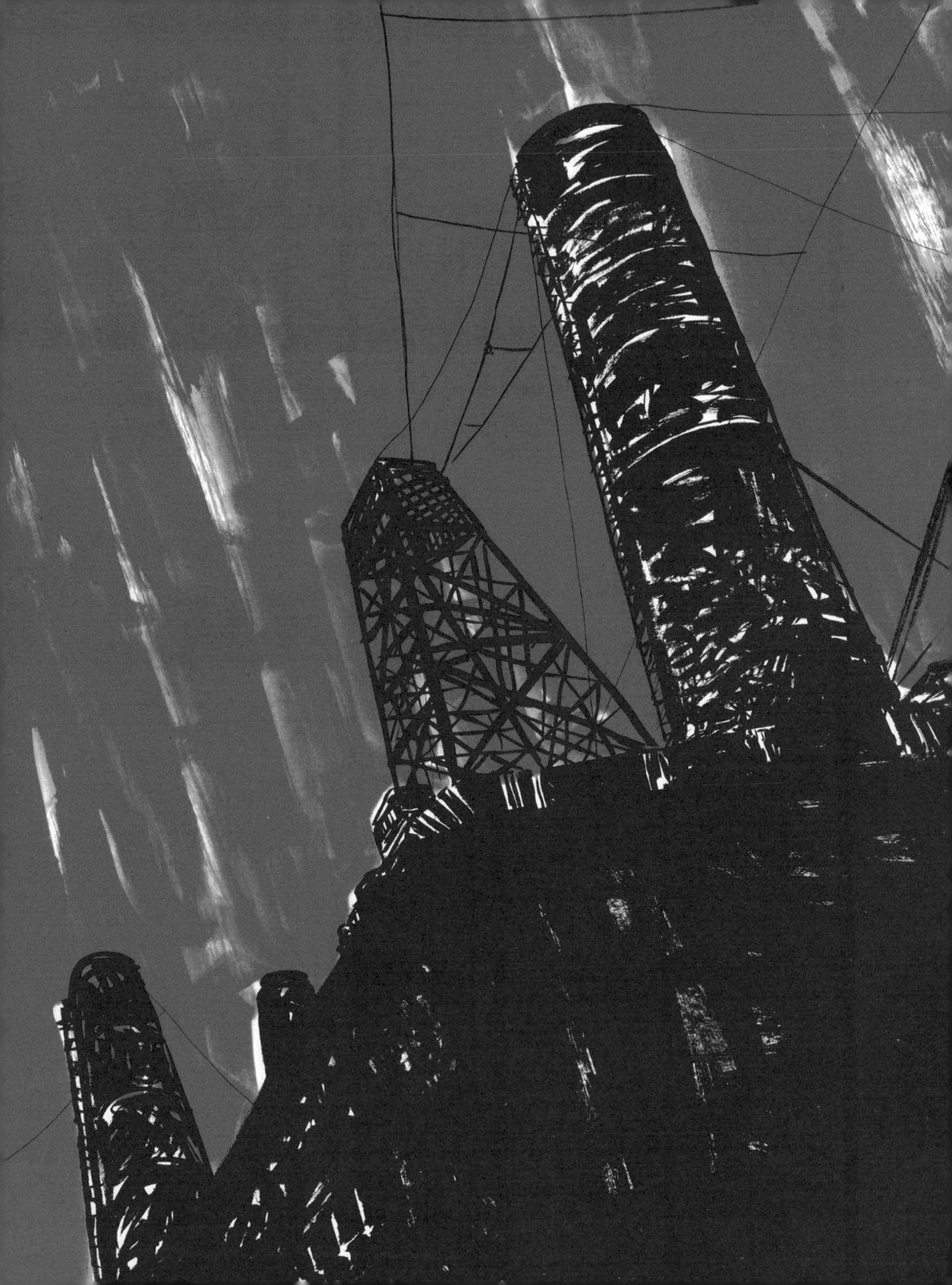

FOR OUR STRUGGLE
IS NOT AGAINST
FLESH AND BLOOD,
BUT AGAINST THE
RULERS AGAINST
THE *AUTHORITIES*,
AGAINST THE
*POWERS OF THIS
DARK WORLD,* AND
AGAINST THE
SPIRITUAL FORCES
OF *EVIL* IN THE
HEAVENLY REALM

Ephesians 6:12

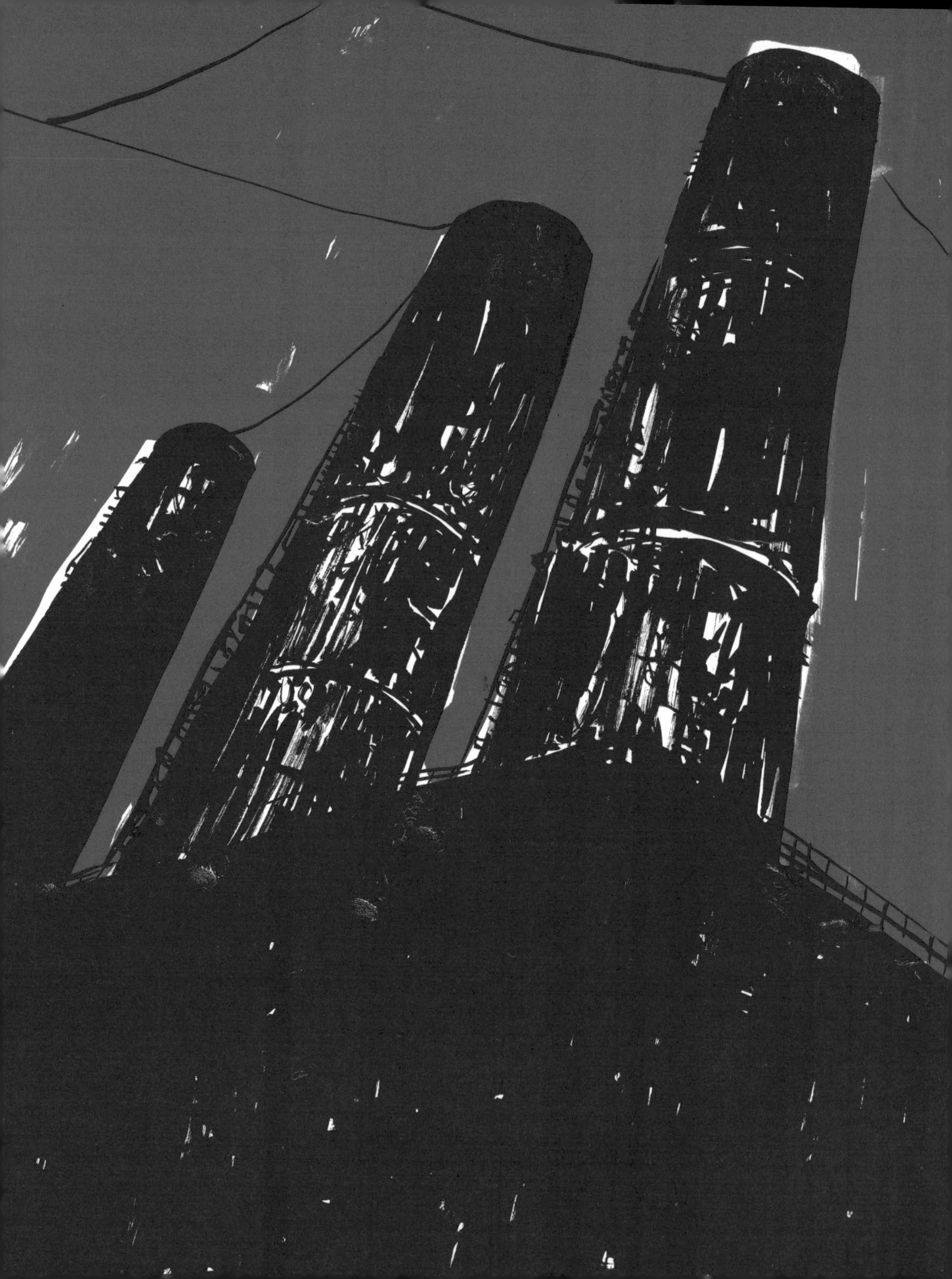

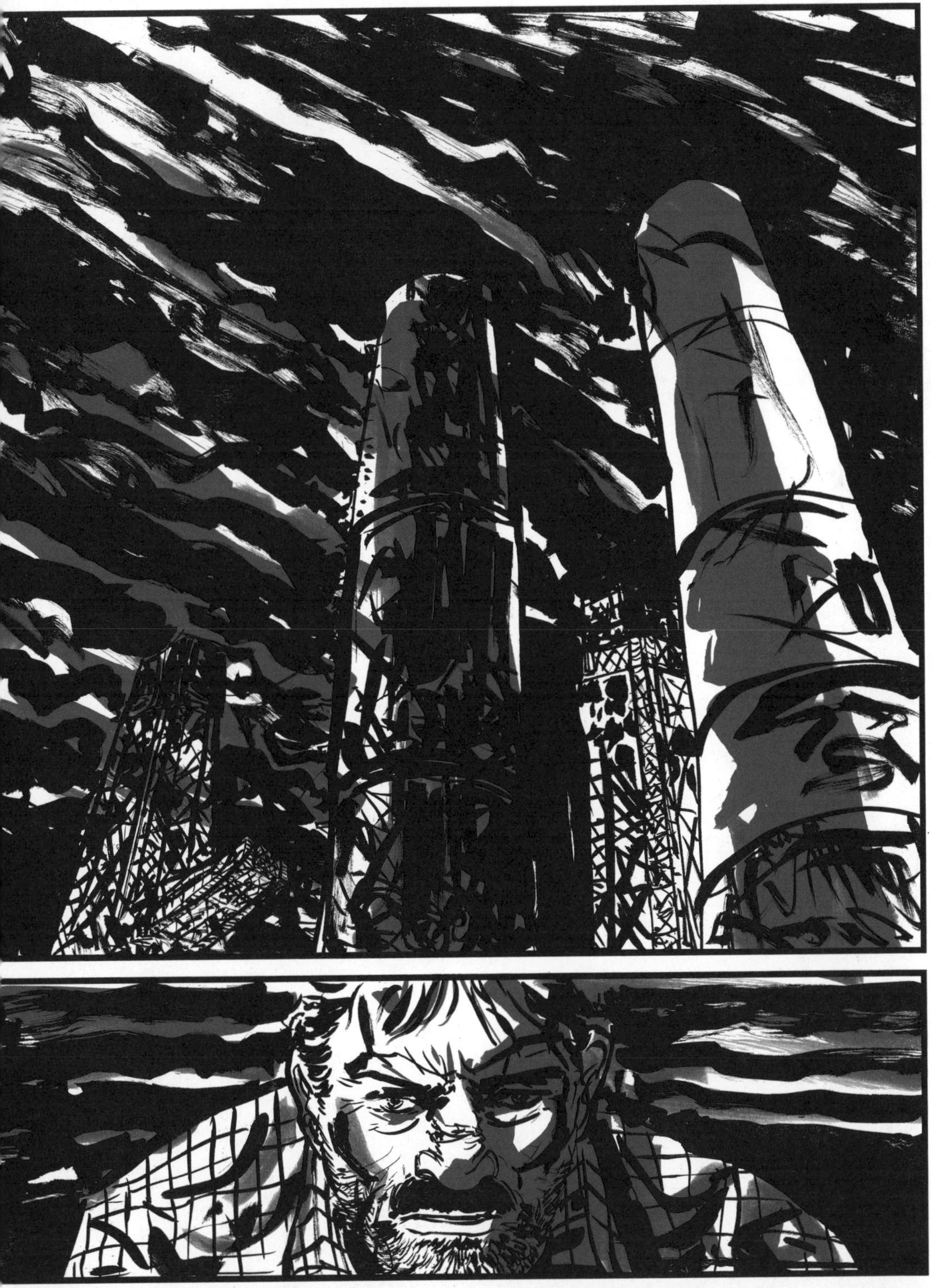

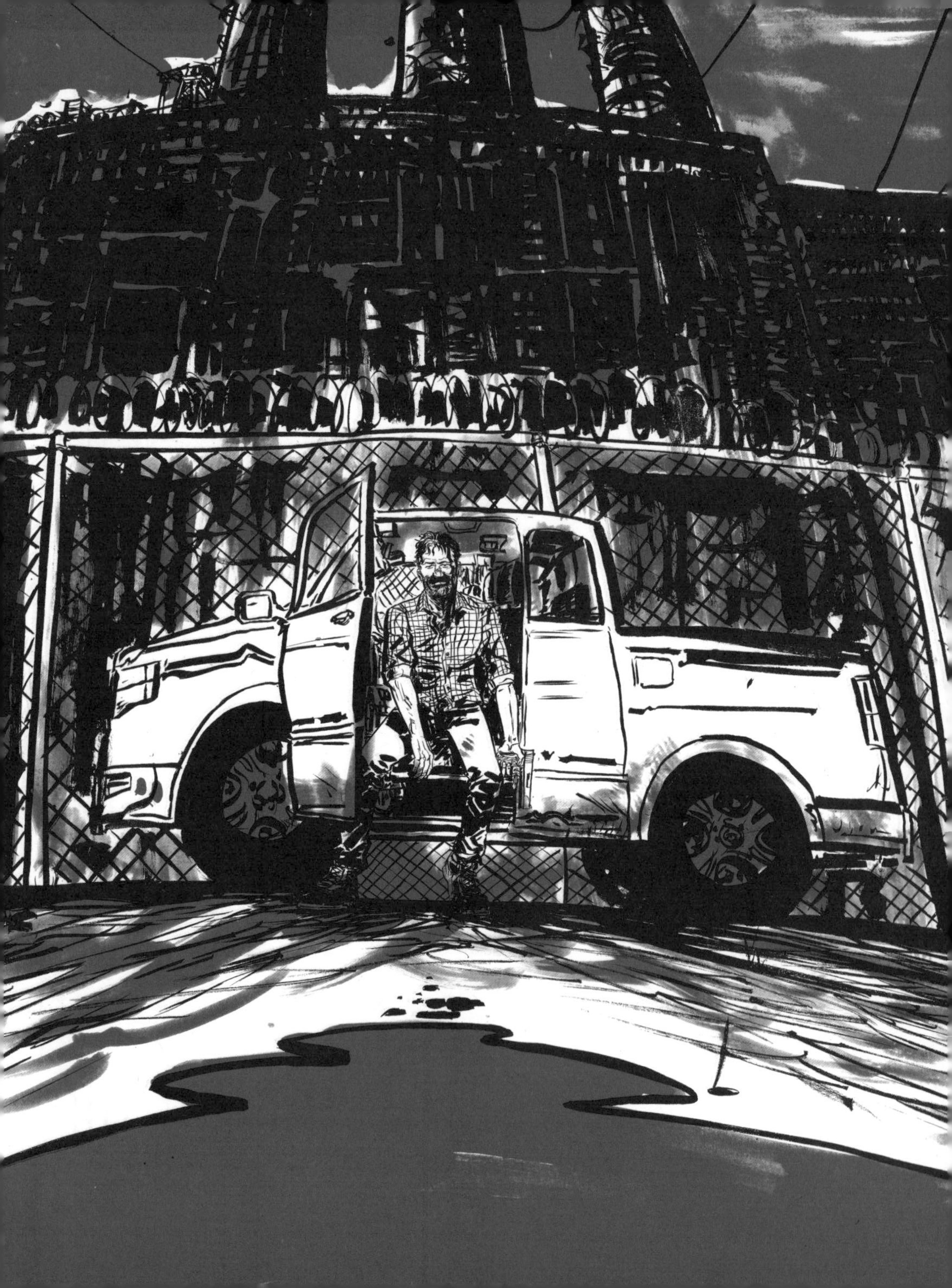

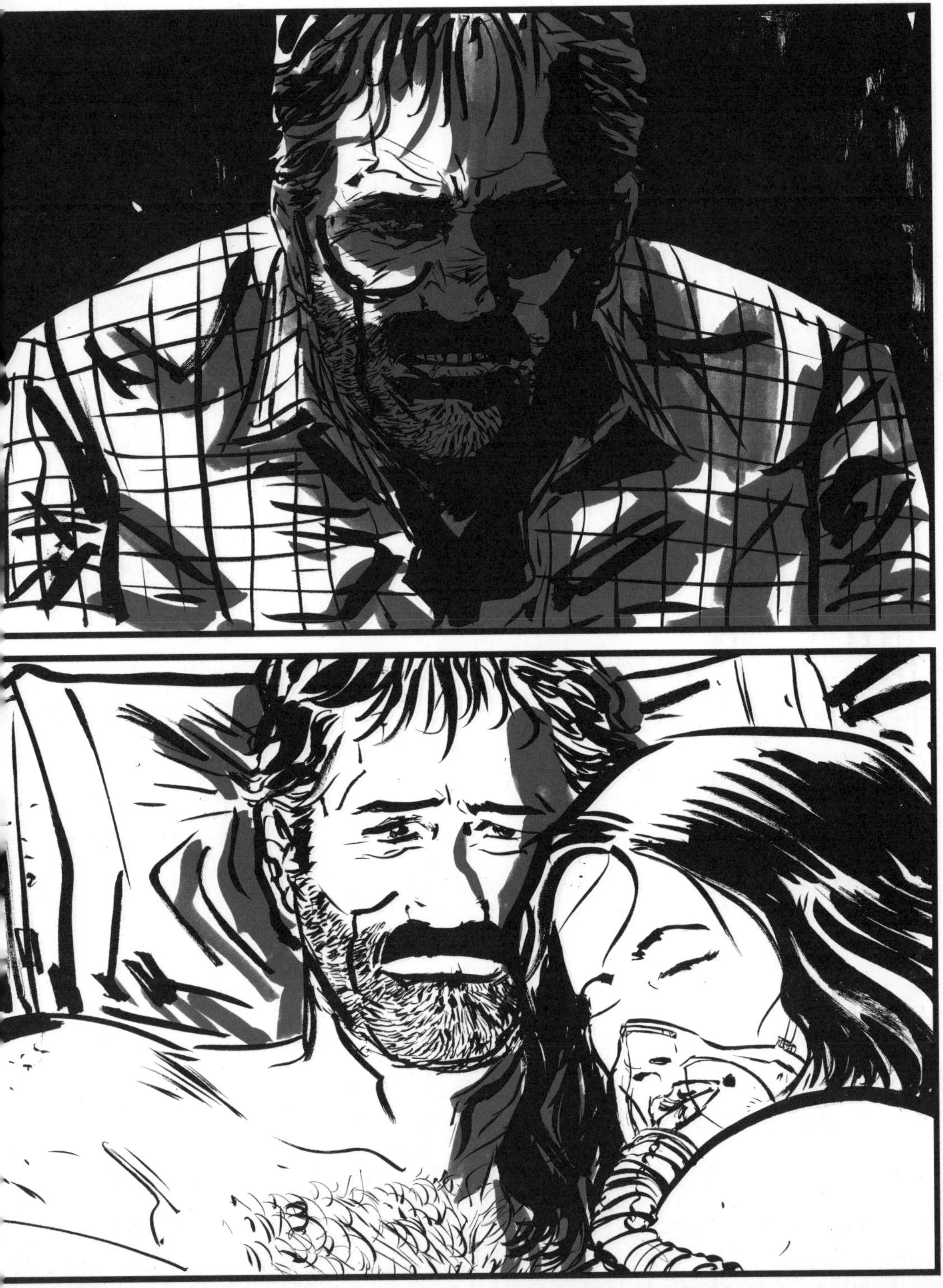

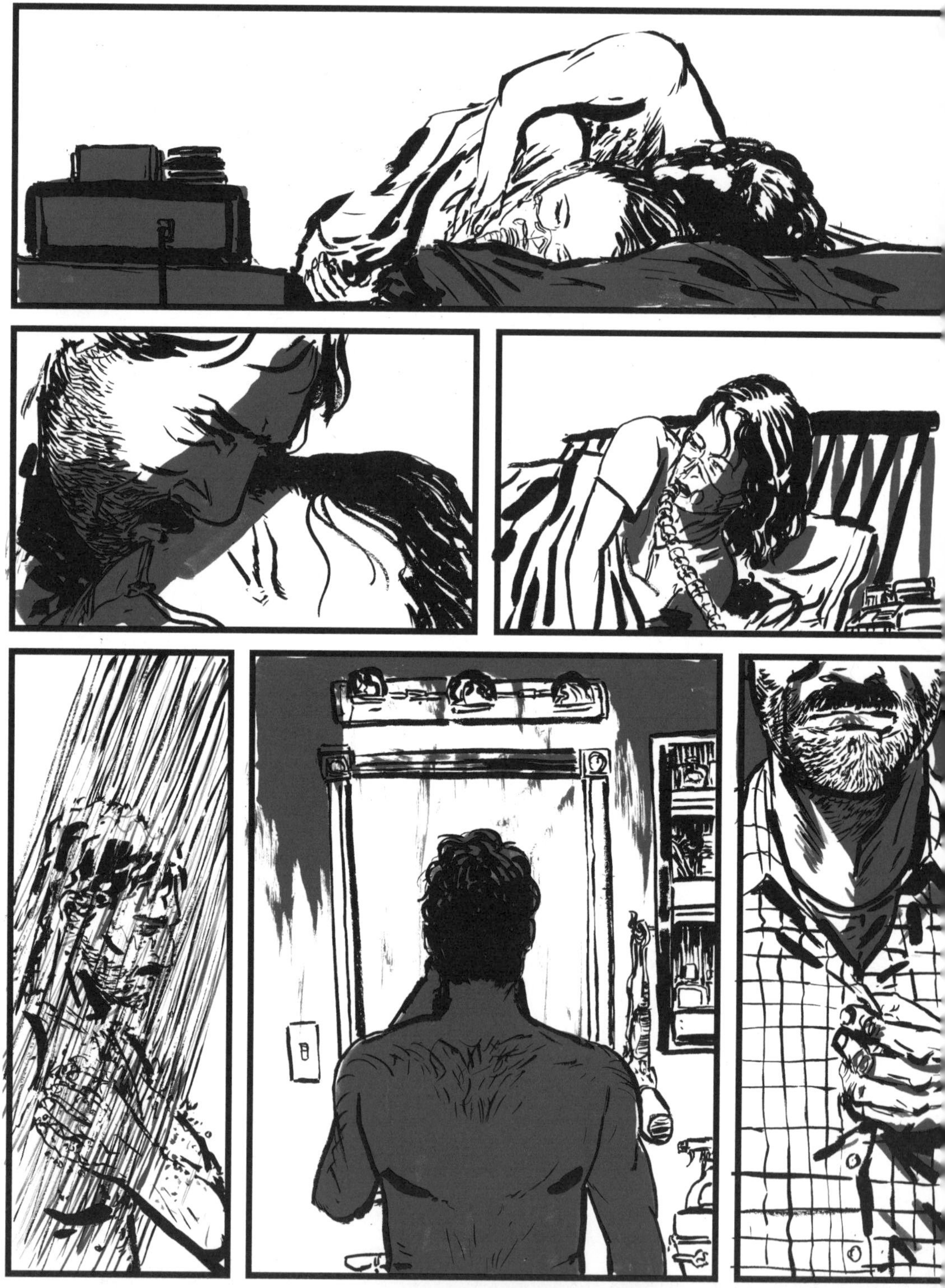

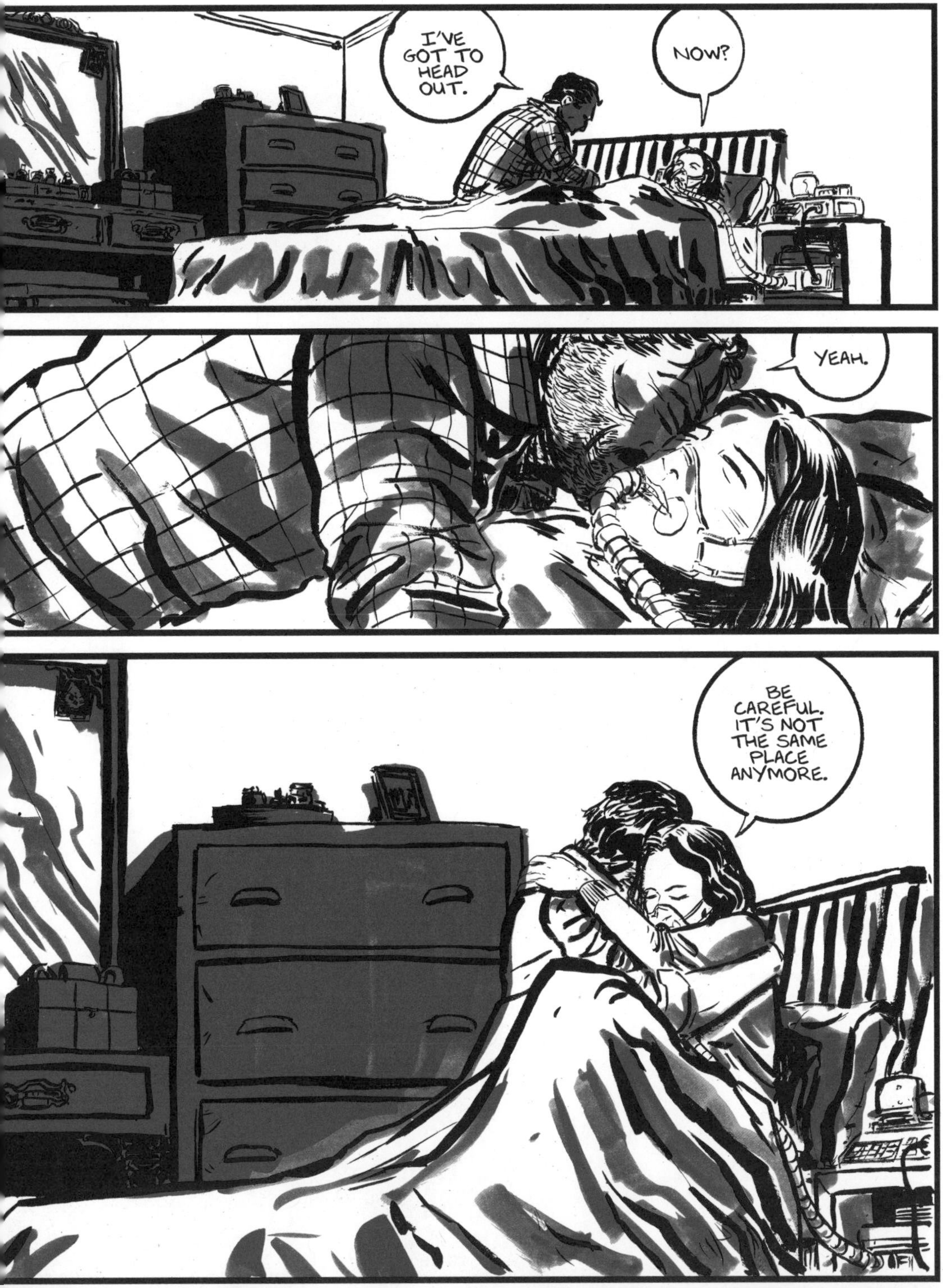
I'VE GOT TO HEAD OUT.
NOW?
YEAH.
BE CAREFUL. IT'S NOT THE SAME PLACE ANYMORE.

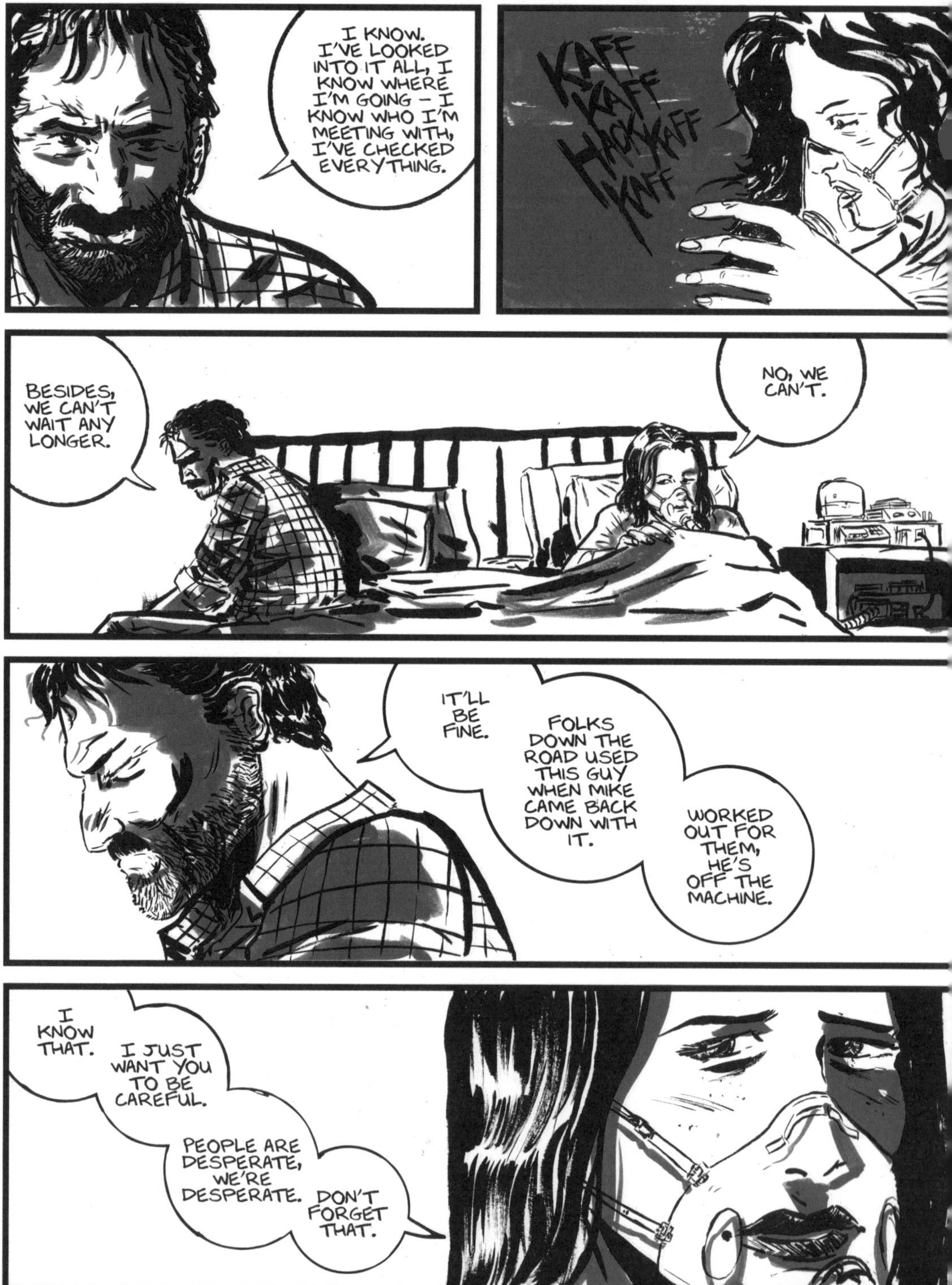
I KNOW. I'VE LOOKED INTO IT ALL, I KNOW WHERE I'M GOING – I KNOW WHO I'M MEETING WITH, I'VE CHECKED EVERYTHING.
KAFF KAFF HACK KAFF KAFF
BESIDES, WE CAN'T WAIT ANY LONGER.
NO, WE CAN'T.
IT'LL BE FINE.
FOLKS DOWN THE ROAD USED THIS GUY WHEN MIKE CAME BACK DOWN WITH IT.
WORKED OUT FOR THEM, HE'S OFF THE MACHINE.
I KNOW THAT.
I JUST WANT YOU TO BE CAREFUL.
PEOPLE ARE DESPERATE, WE'RE DESPERATE.
DON'T FORGET THAT.

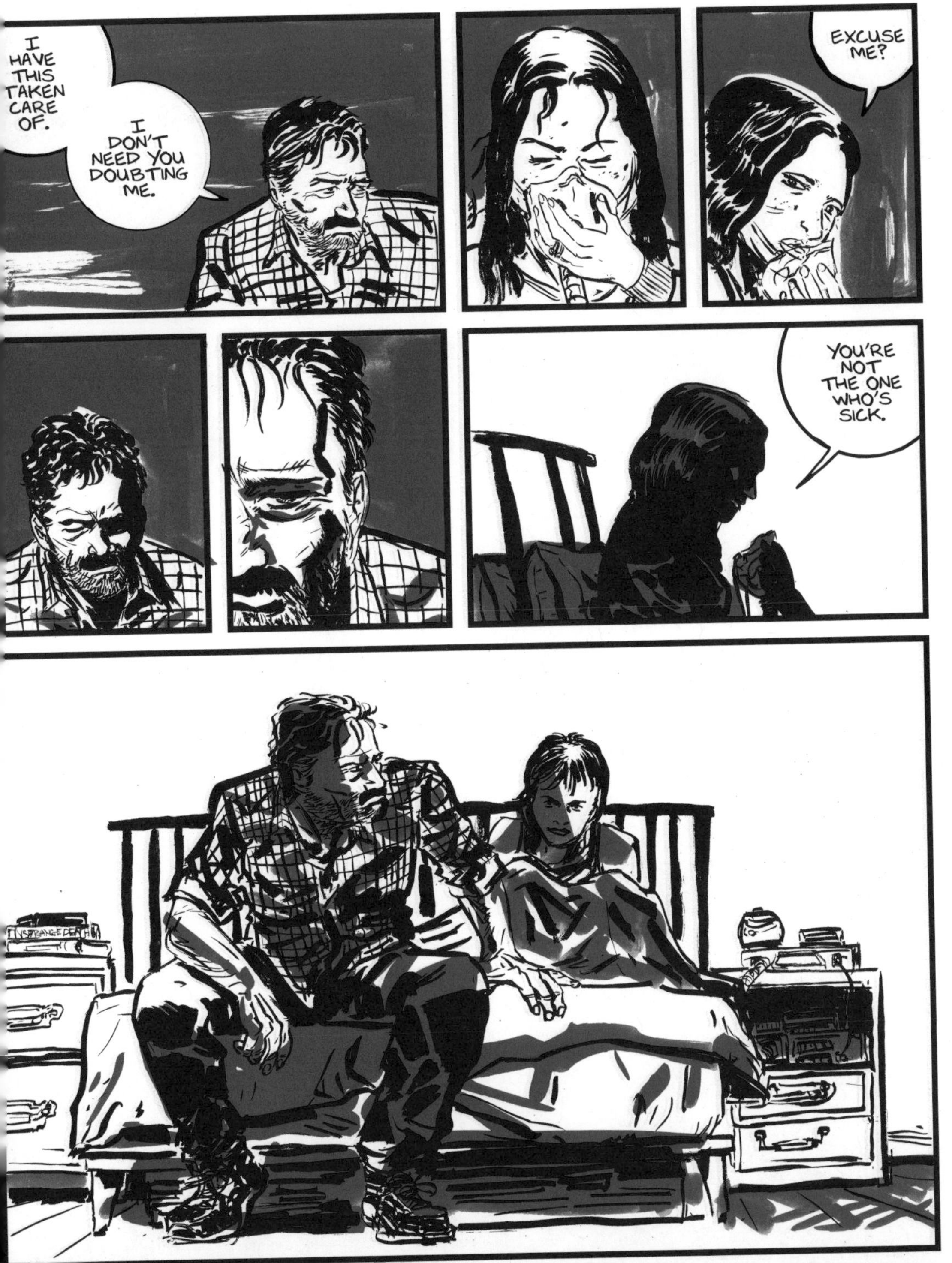
I HAVE THIS TAKEN CARE OF.
I DON'T NEED YOU DOUBTING ME.
EXCUSE ME?
YOU'RE NOT THE ONE WHO'S SICK.

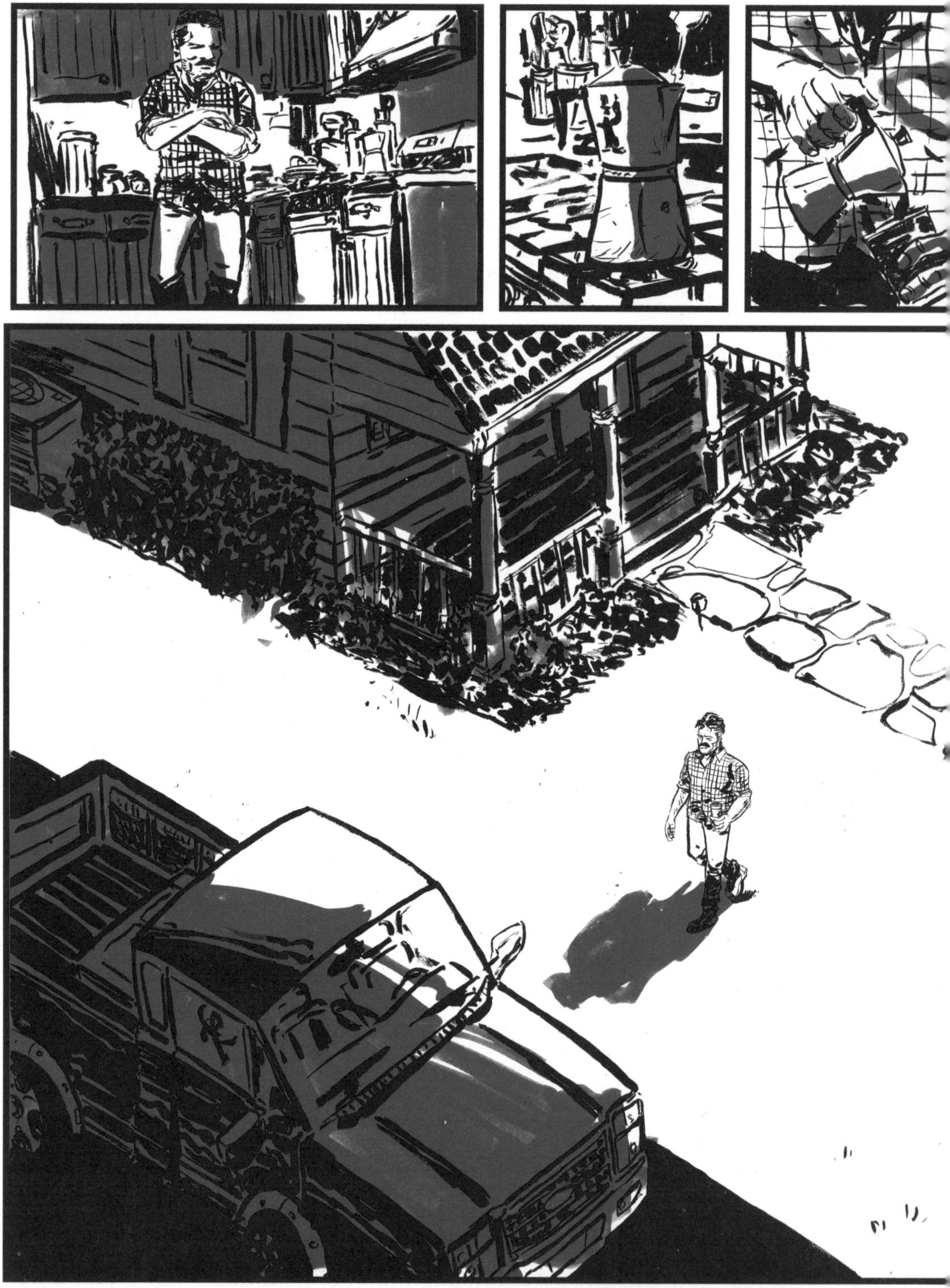

...THAT WAS 'GIRL IN THE WAR' BY JOSH RITTER...

...HERE ON XPM WE'VE GOT SOME MORE GREAT OLDIES COMING UP...

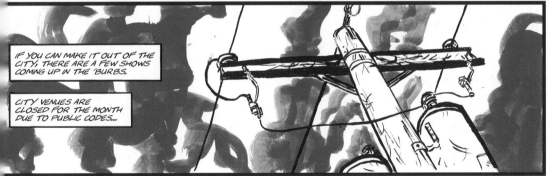

IF YOU CAN MAKE IT OUT OF THE CITY, THERE ARE A FEW SHOWS COMING UP IN THE 'BURBS.

CITY VENUES ARE CLOSED FOR THE MONTH DUE TO PUBLIC CODES...

HERE'S CORY BRANAN WITH 'THAT LOOK I LOST'

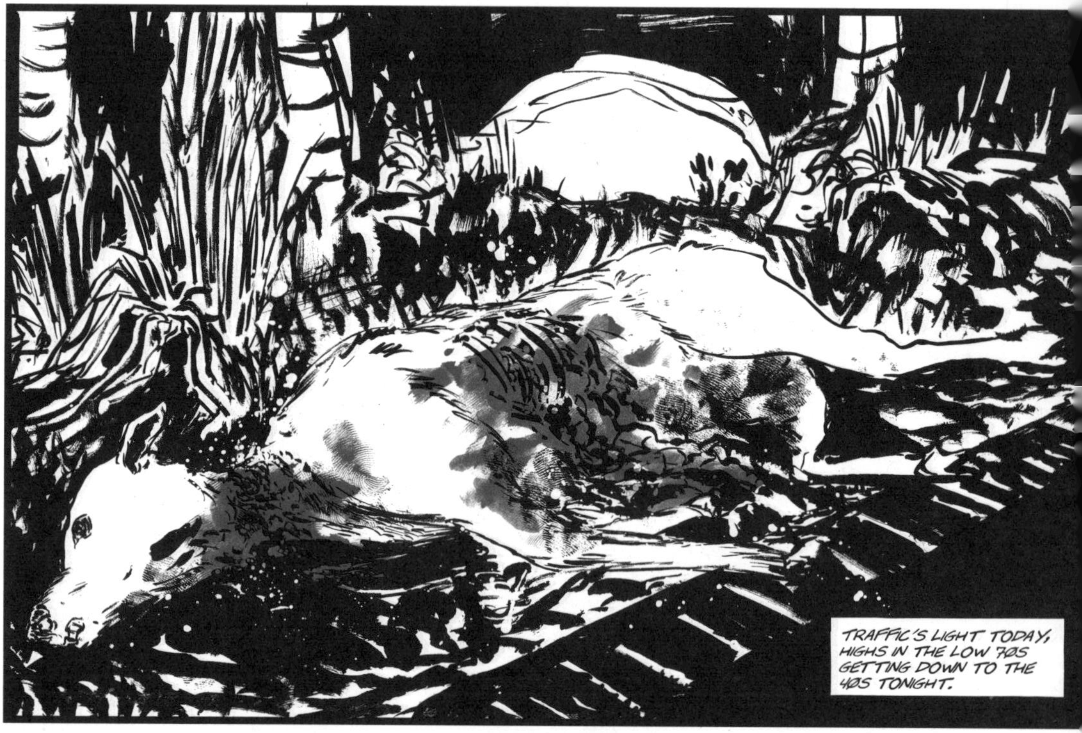
TRAFFIC'S LIGHT TODAY, HIGHS IN THE LOW 70S GETTING DOWN TO THE 40S TONIGHT.

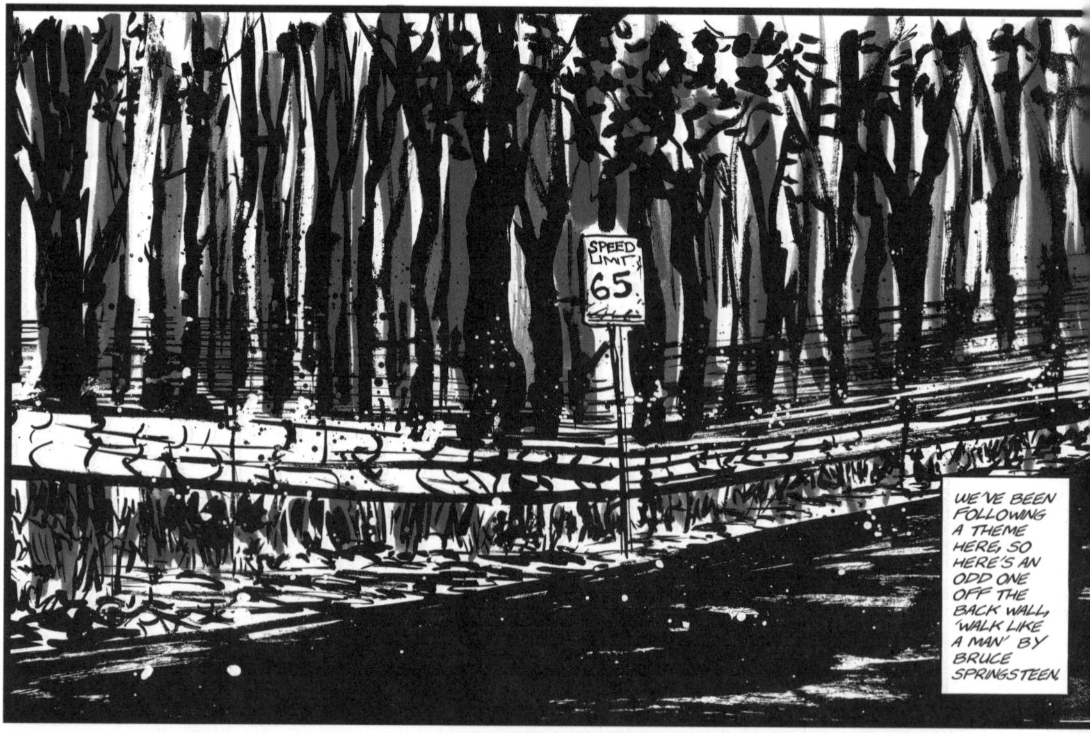
SPEED LIMIT 65
WE'VE BEEN FOLLOWING A THEME HERE, SO HERE'S AN ODD ONE OFF THE BACK WALL, 'WALK LIKE A MAN' BY BRUCE SPRINGSTEEN.

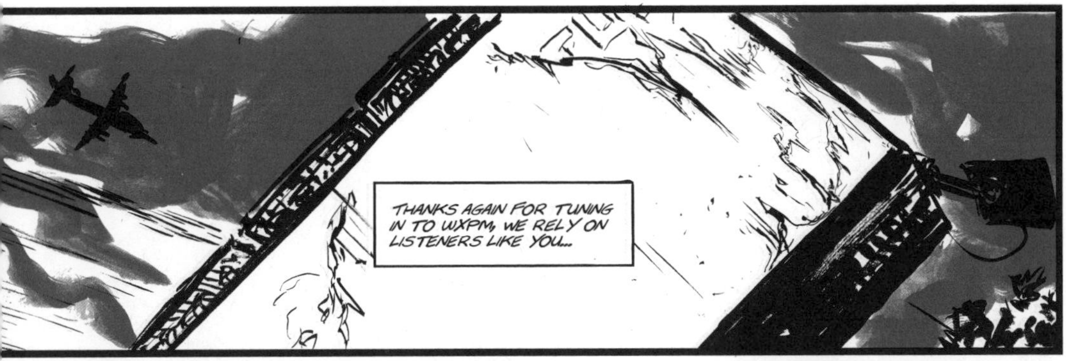
THANKS AGAIN FOR TUNING IN TO WXPM, WE RELY ON LISTENERS LIKE YOU...

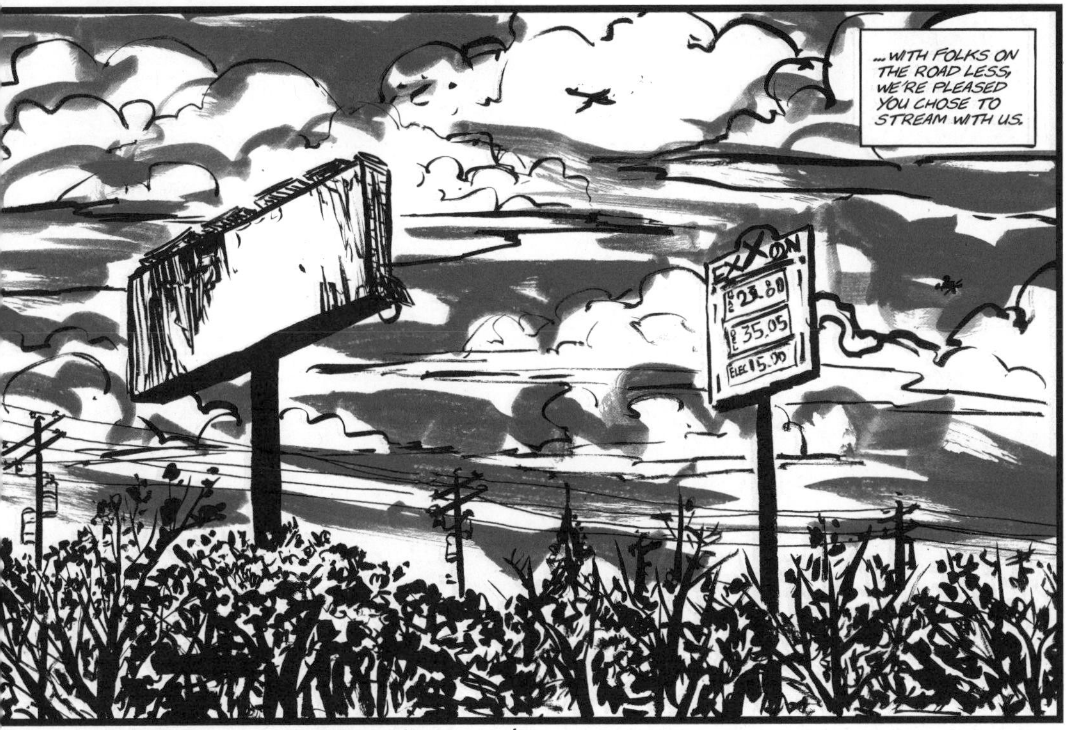
...WITH FOLKS ON THE ROAD LESS, WE'RE PLEASED YOU CHOSE TO STREAM WITH US.

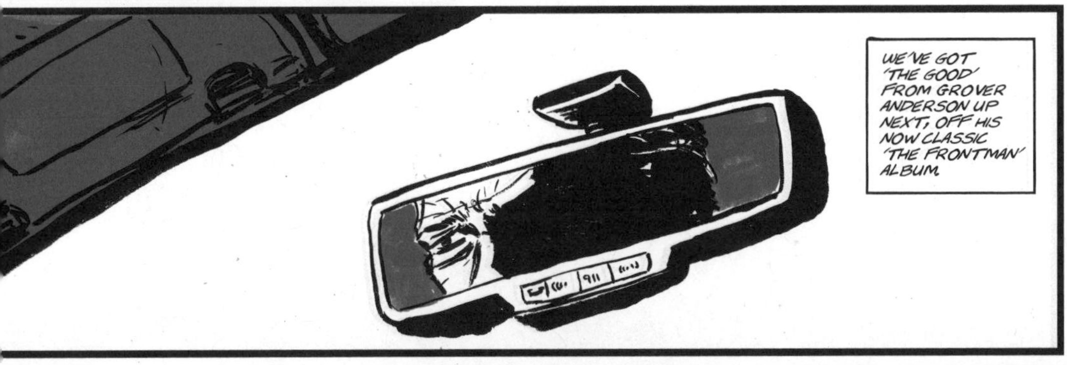
WE'VE GOT 'THE GOOD' FROM GROVER ANDERSON UP NEXT, OFF HIS NOW CLASSIC 'THE FRONTMAN' ALBUM.

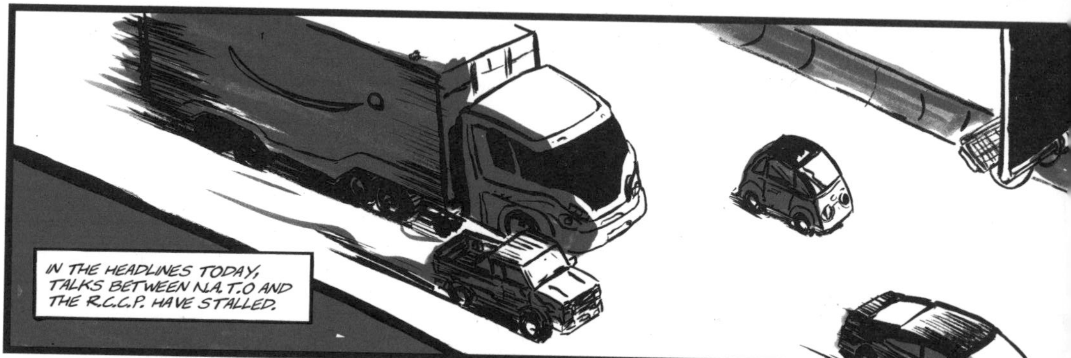
IN THE HEADLINES TODAY, TALKS BETWEEN N.A.T.O AND THE R.C.C.P. HAVE STALLED.

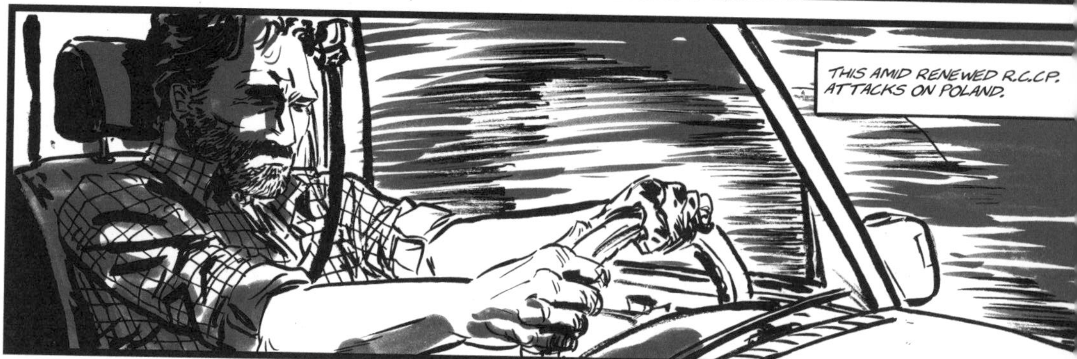
THIS AMID RENEWED R.C.C.P. ATTACKS ON POLAND.

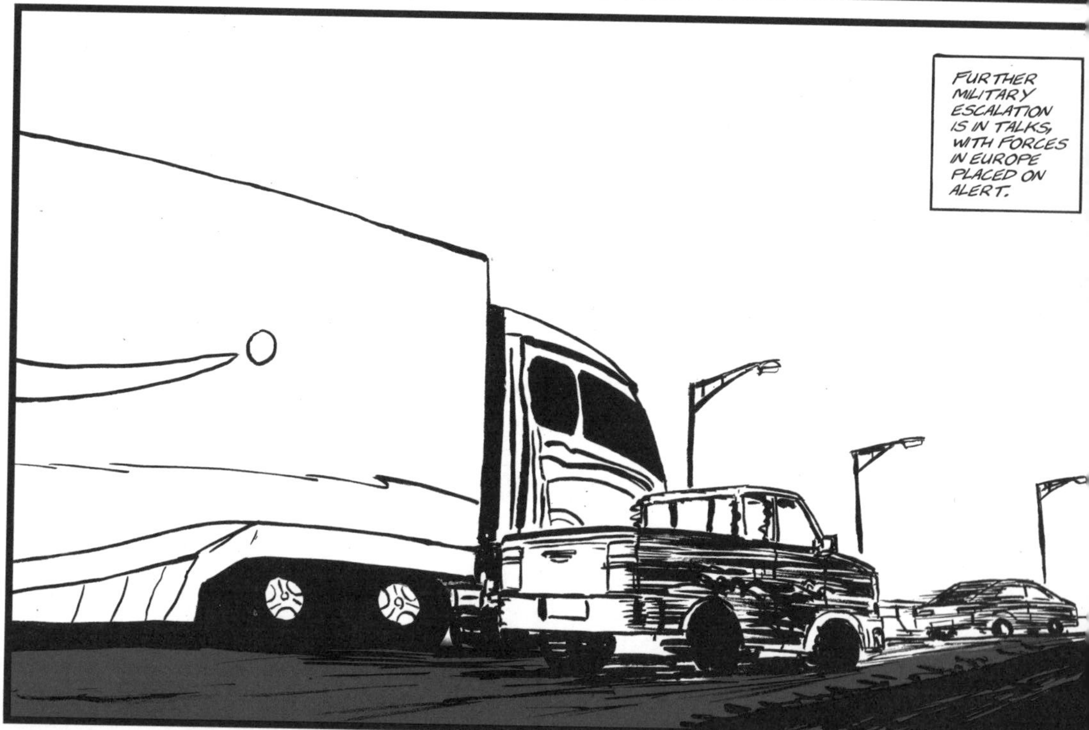
FURTHER MILITARY ESCALATION IS IN TALKS, WITH FORCES IN EUROPE PLACED ON ALERT.

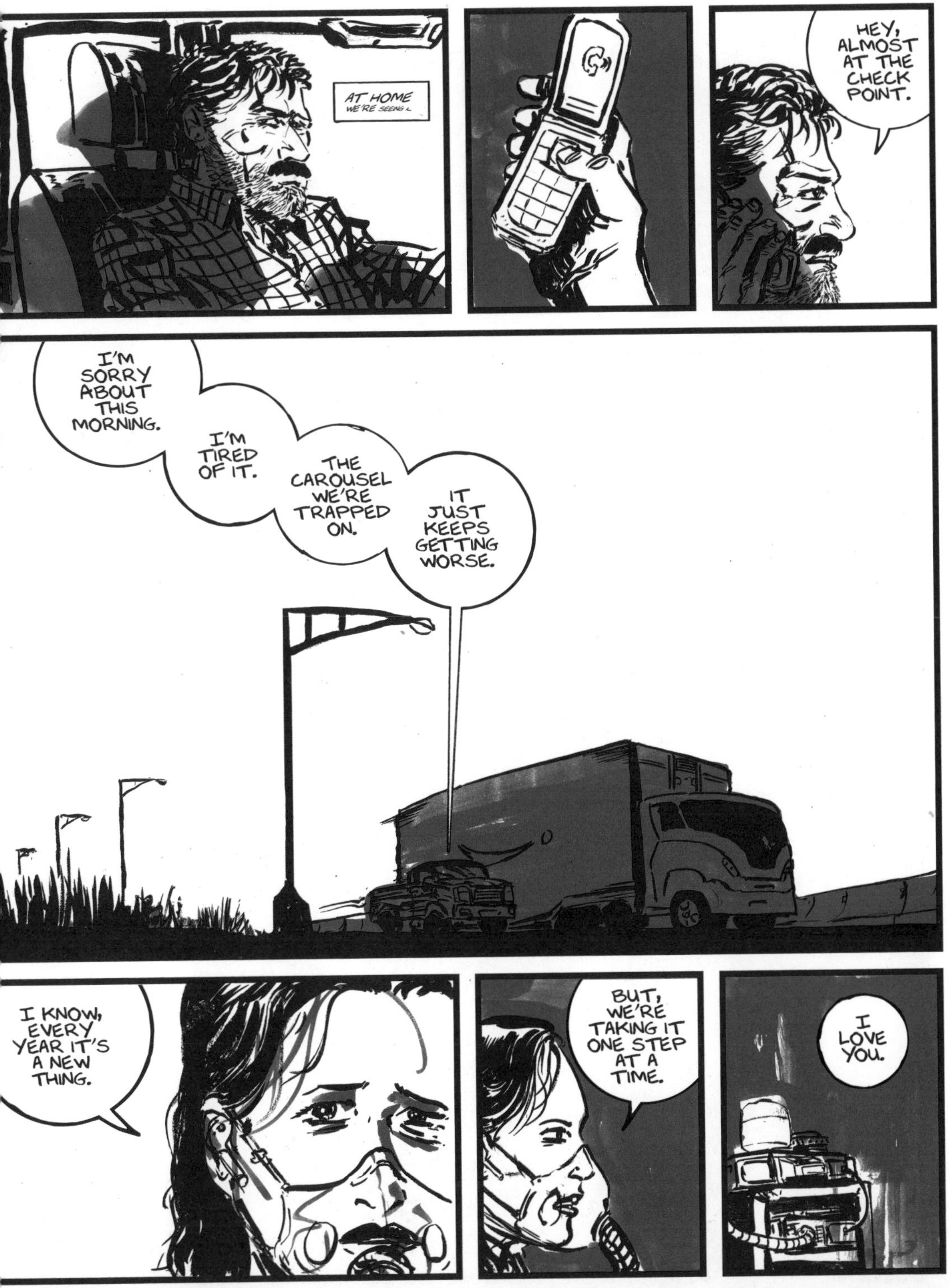
AT HOME WE'RE SEEING
HEY, ALMOST AT THE CHECK POINT.
I'M SORRY ABOUT THIS MORNING.
I'M TIRED OF IT.
THE CAROUSEL WE'RE TRAPPED ON.
IT JUST KEEPS GETTING WORSE.
I KNOW, EVERY YEAR IT'S A NEW THING.
BUT, WE'RE TAKING IT ONE STEP AT A TIME.
I LOVE YOU.

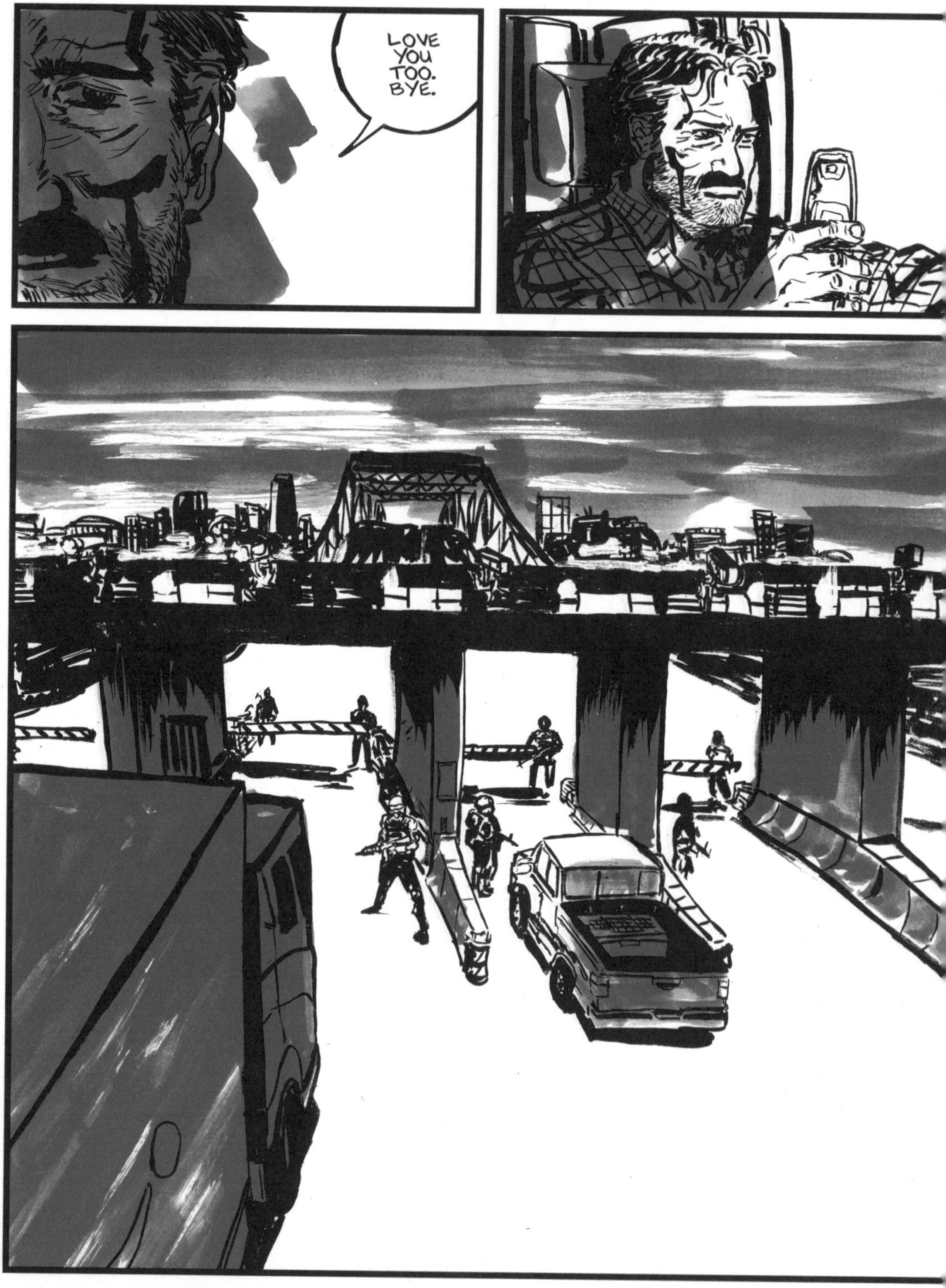
LOVE YOU TOO. BYE.

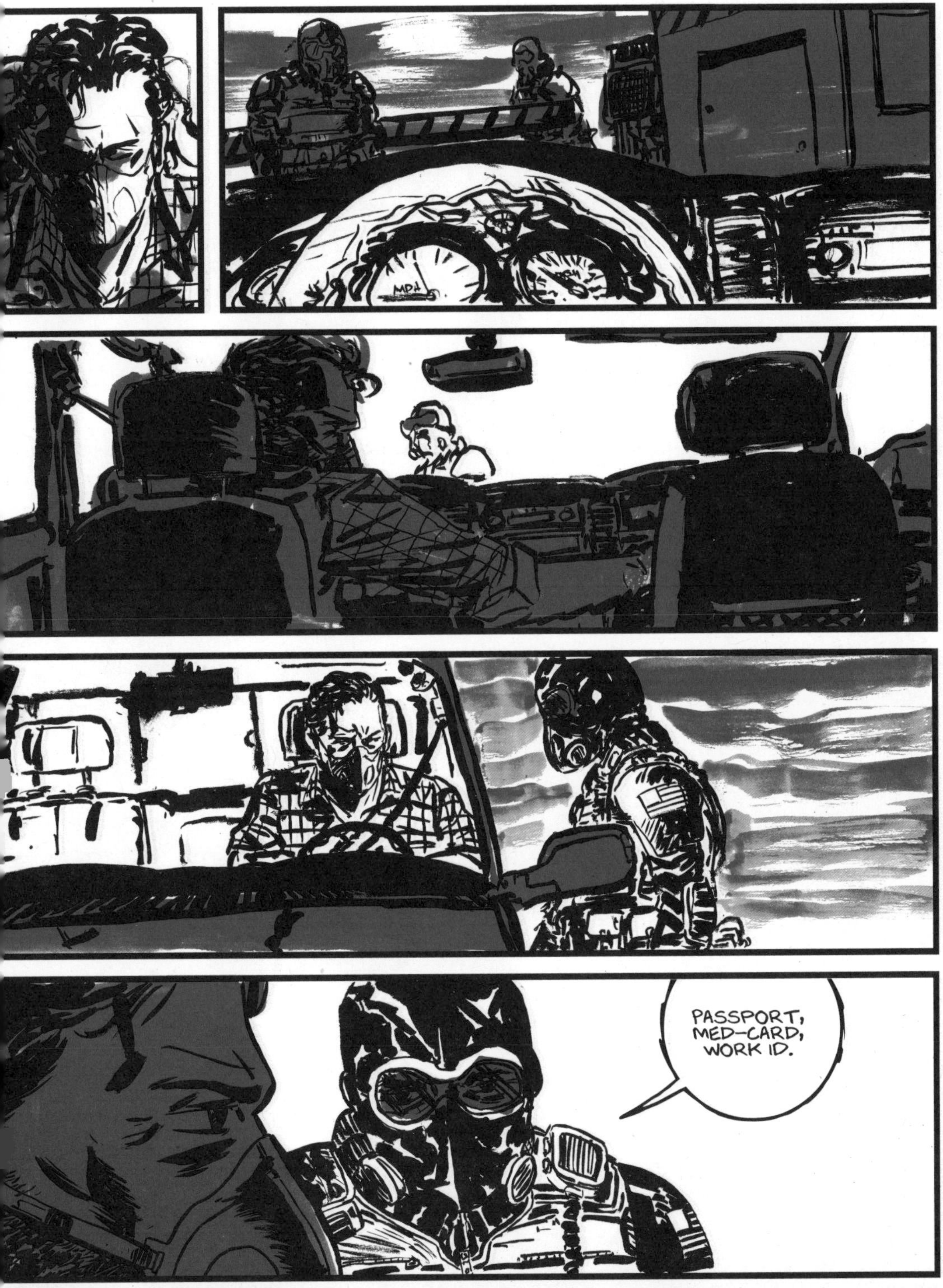
PASSPORT, MED-CARD, WORK ID.

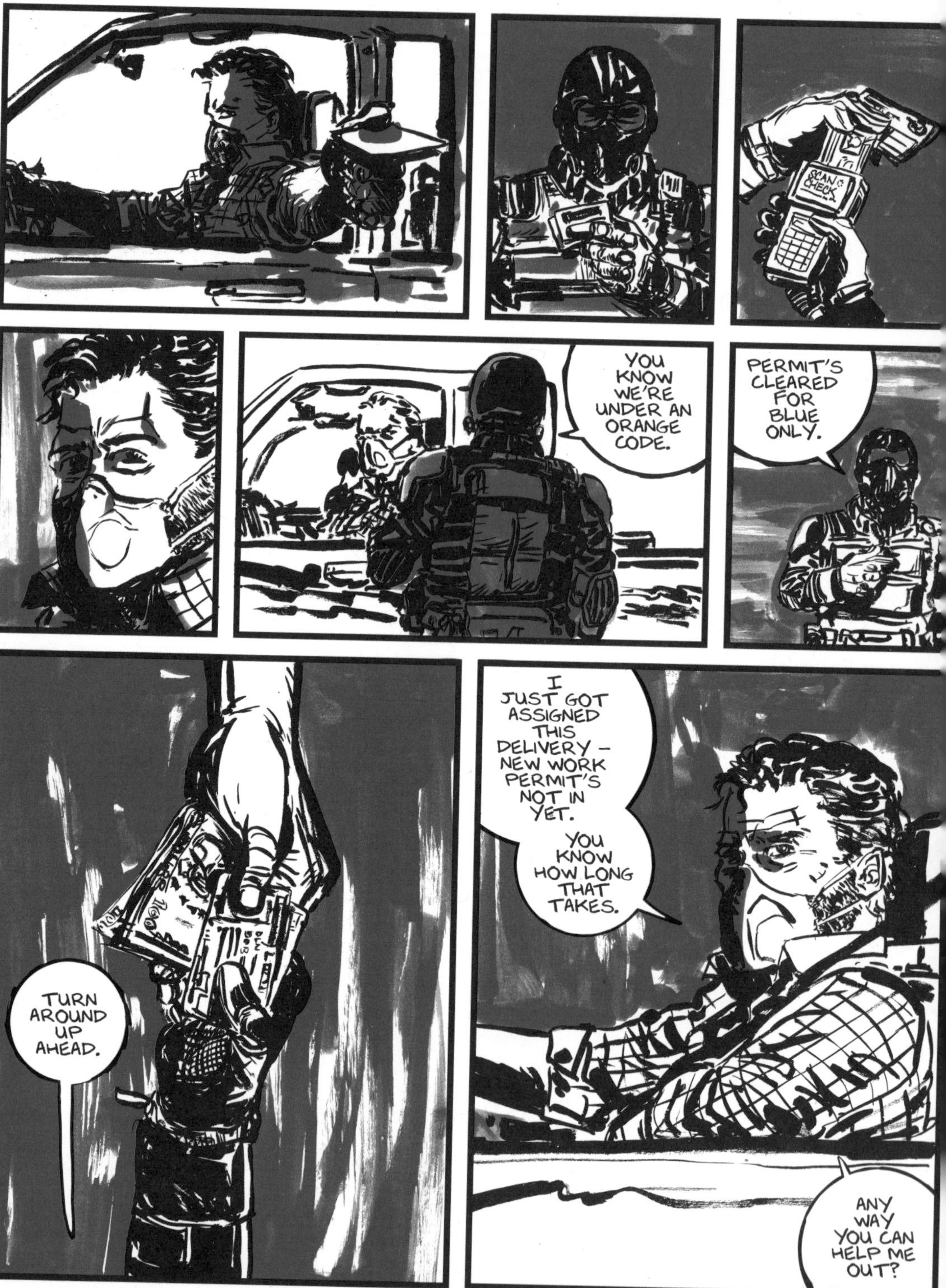
SCAN CHECK
YOU KNOW WE'RE UNDER AN ORANGE CODE.
PERMIT'S CLEARED FOR BLUE ONLY.
I JUST GOT ASSIGNED THIS DELIVERY – NEW WORK PERMIT'S NOT IN YET.
YOU KNOW HOW LONG THAT TAKES.
ANY WAY YOU CAN HELP ME OUT?
TURN AROUND UP AHEAD.

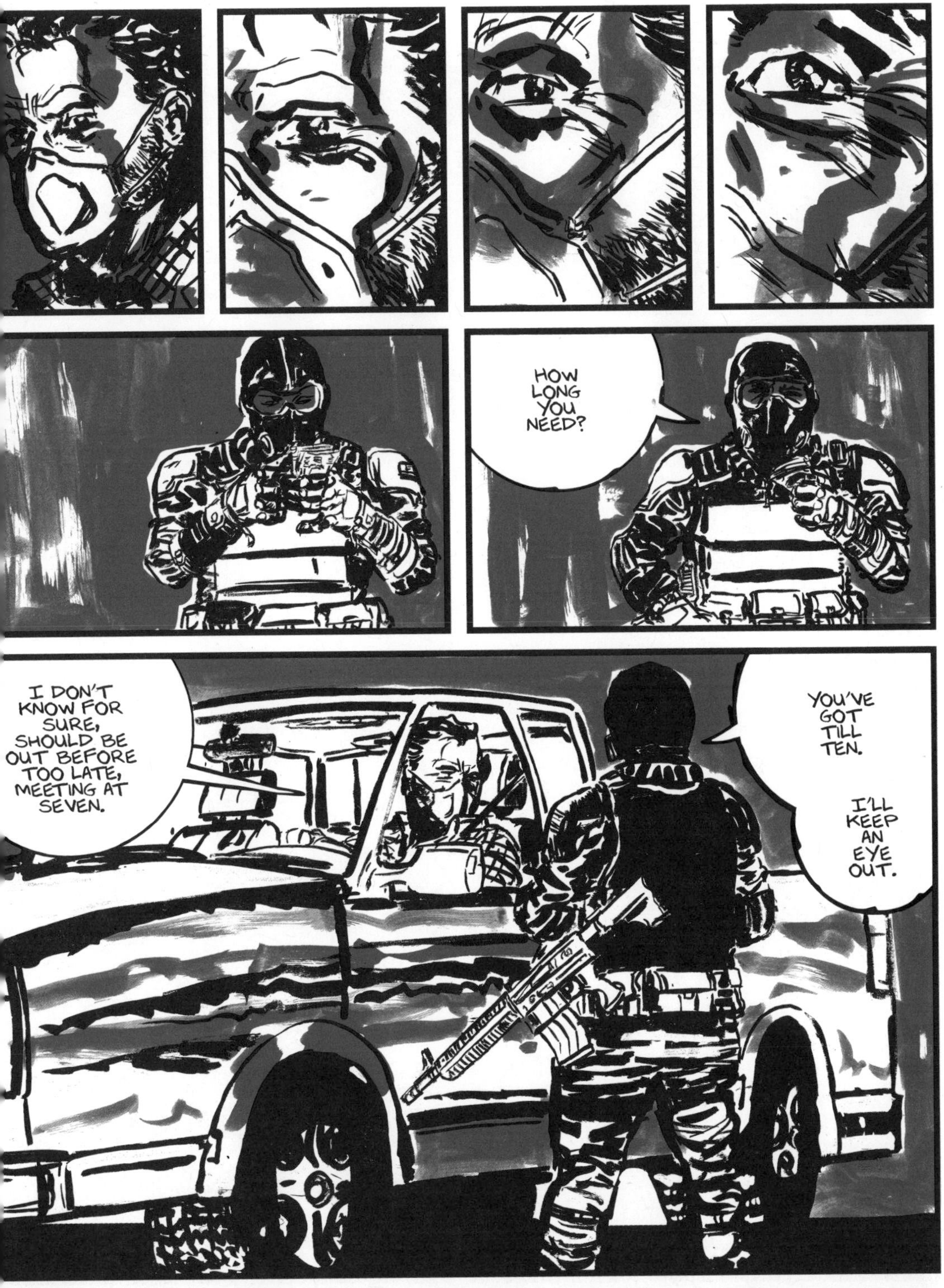
HOW LONG YOU NEED?
I DON'T KNOW FOR SURE, SHOULD BE OUT BEFORE TOO LATE, MEETING AT SEVEN.
YOU'VE GOT TILL TEN.
I'LL KEEP AN EYE OUT.

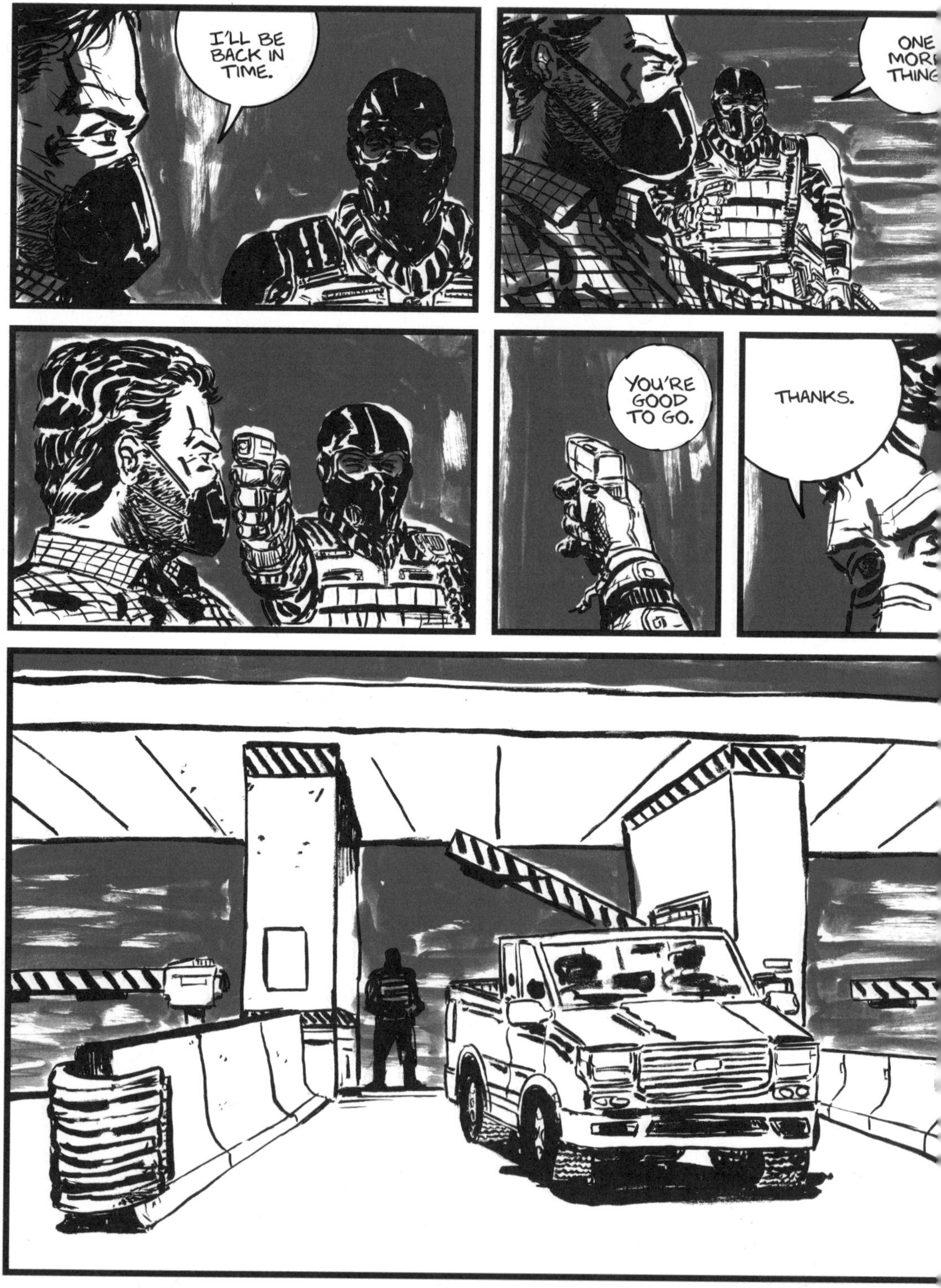
I'LL BE BACK IN TIME.
ONE MOR THING
YOU'RE GOOD TO GO.
THANKS.

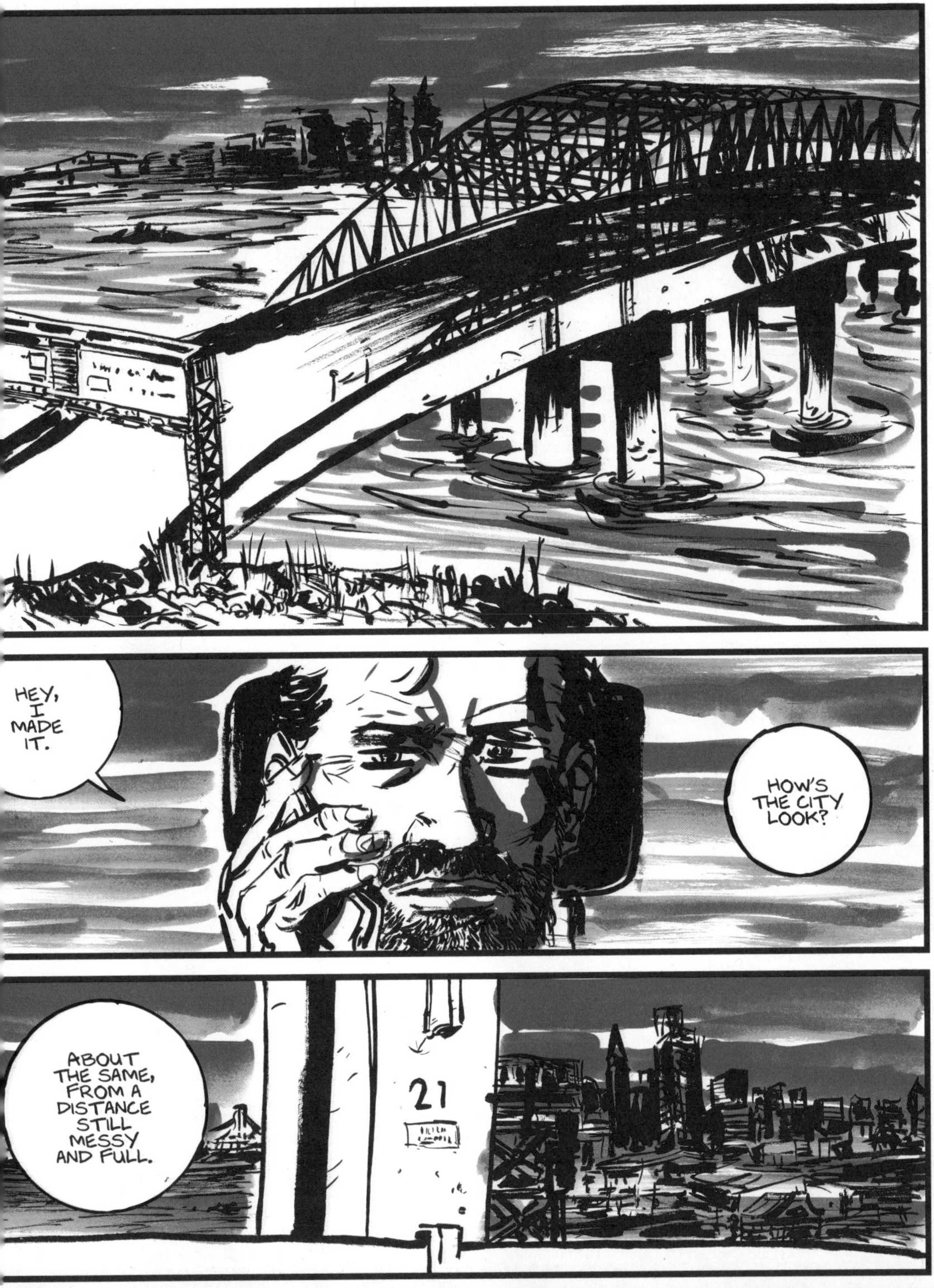
HEY, I MADE IT.
HOW'S THE CITY LOOK?
ABOUT THE SAME, FROM A DISTANCE STILL MESSY AND FULL.
21

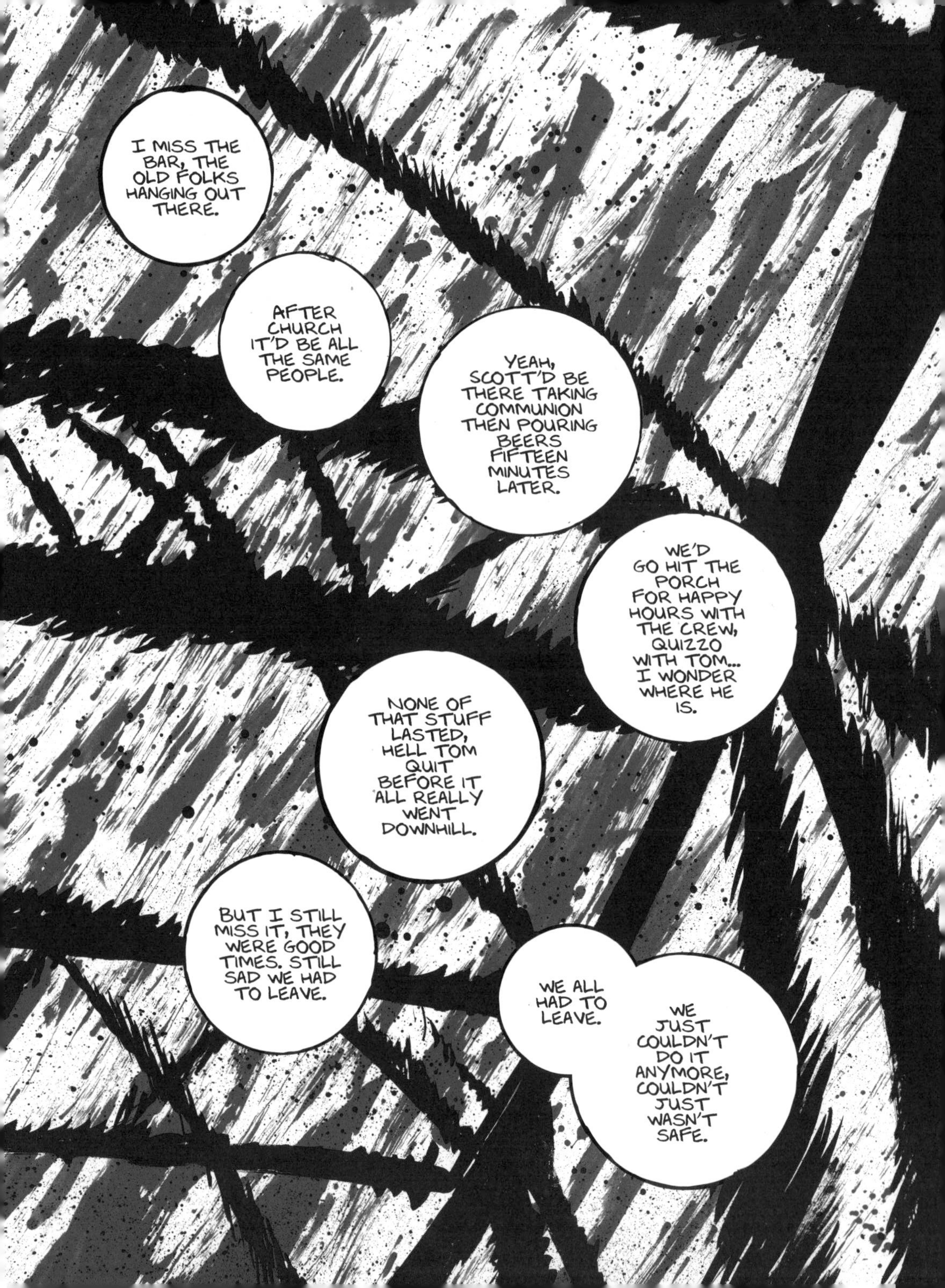
I MISS THE BAR, THE OLD FOLKS HANGING OUT THERE.
AFTER CHURCH IT'D BE ALL THE SAME PEOPLE.
YEAH, SCOTT'D BE THERE TAKING COMMUNION THEN POURING BEERS FIFTEEN MINUTES LATER.
WE'D GO HIT THE PORCH FOR HAPPY HOURS WITH THE CREW, QUIZZO WITH TOM... I WONDER WHERE HE IS.
NONE OF THAT STUFF LASTED, HELL TOM QUIT BEFORE IT ALL REALLY WENT DOWNHILL.
BUT I STILL MISS IT, THEY WERE GOOD TIMES. STILL SAD WE HAD TO LEAVE.
WE ALL HAD TO LEAVE.
WE JUST COULDN'T DO IT ANYMORE, COULDN'T JUST WASN'T SAFE.

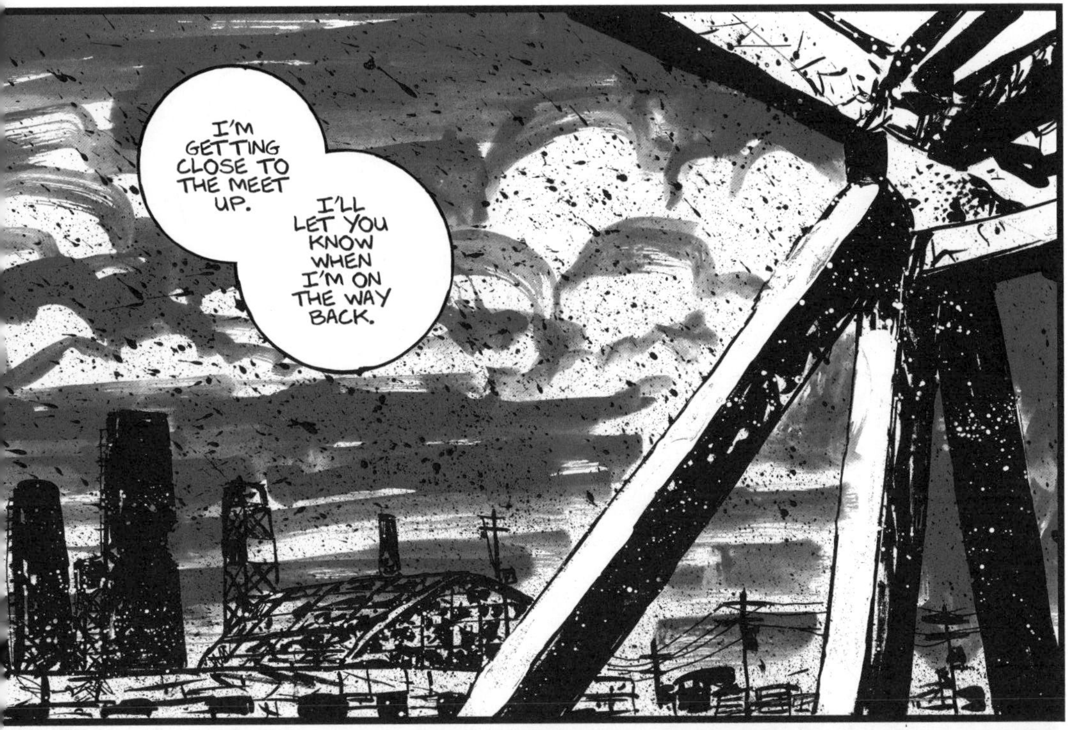
I'M GETTING CLOSE TO THE MEET UP.
I'LL LET YOU KNOW WHEN I'M ON THE WAY BACK.

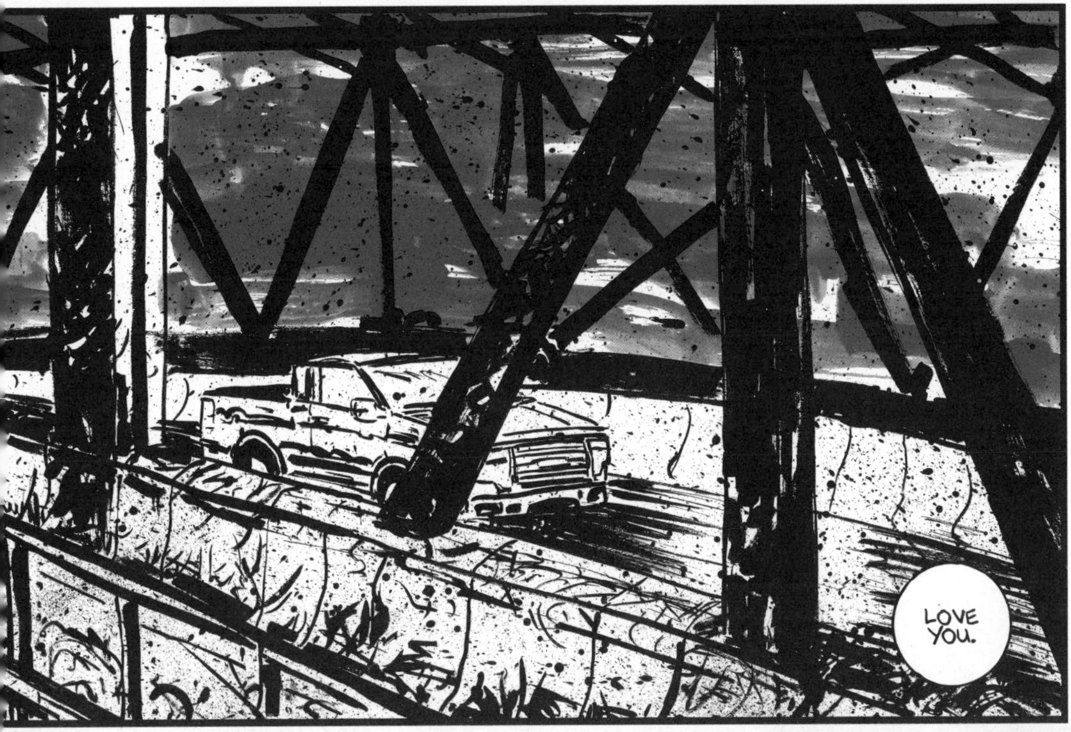
LOVE YOU.

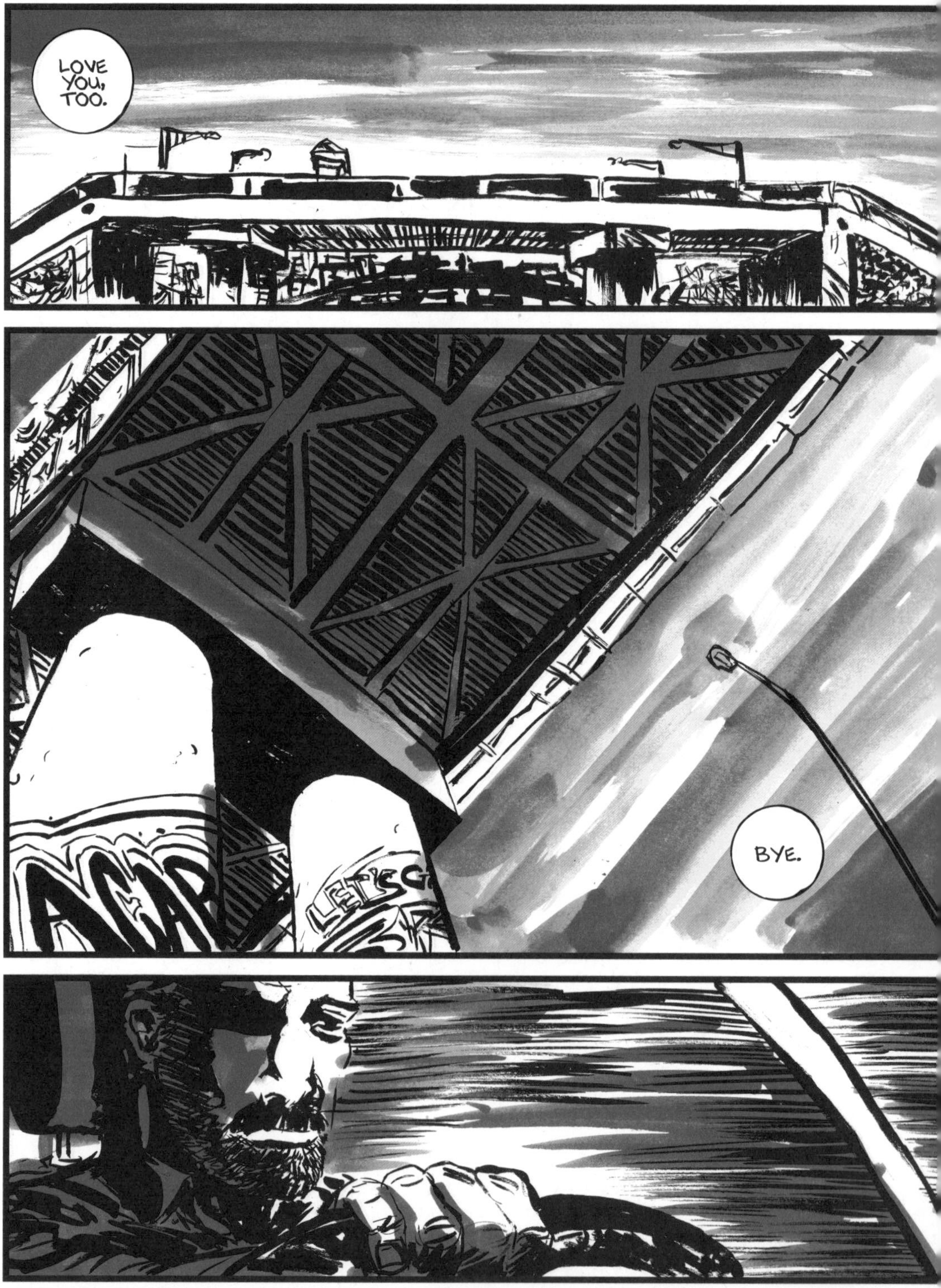
LOVE YOU, TOO.
BYE.

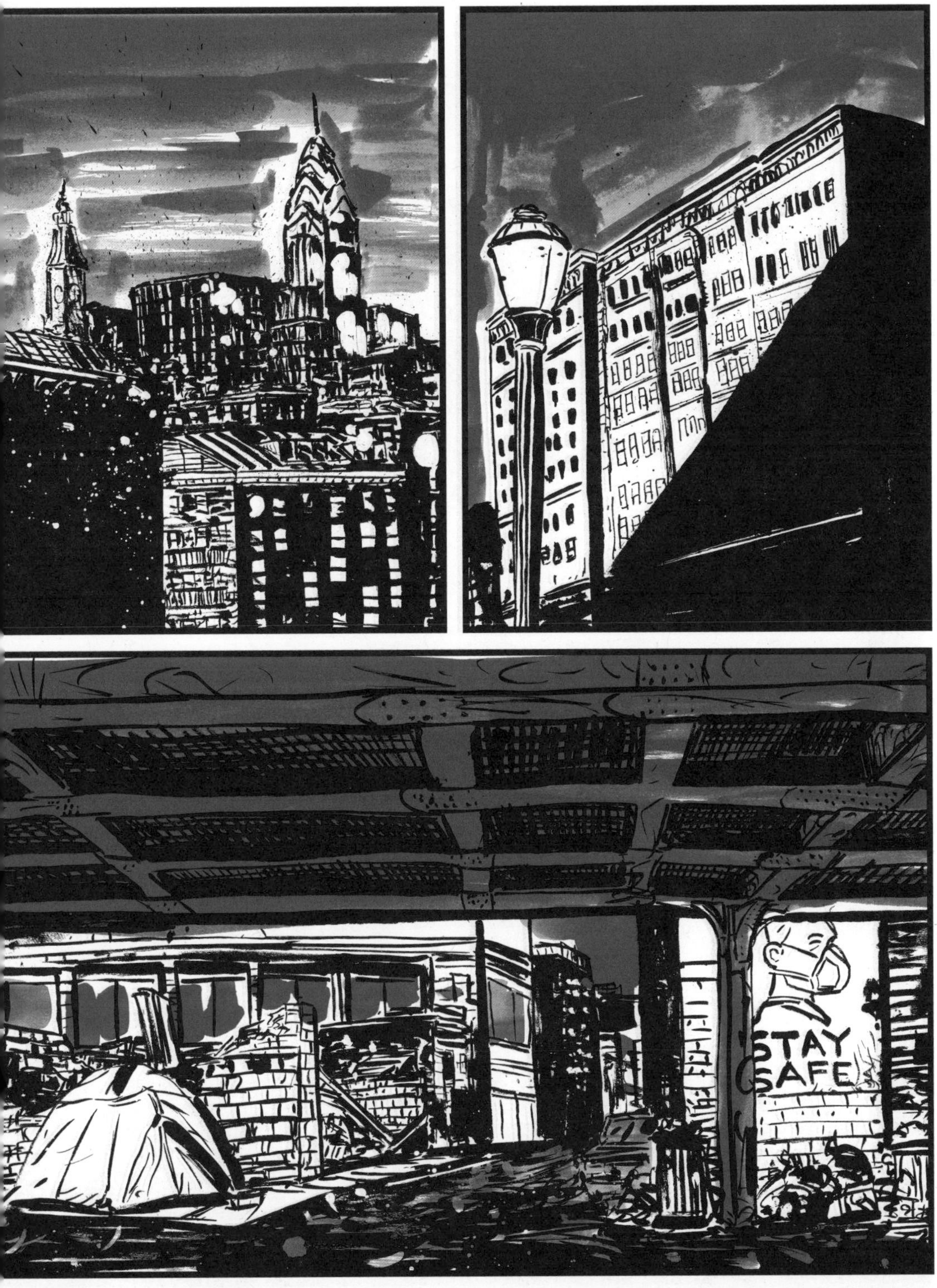
STAY SAFE

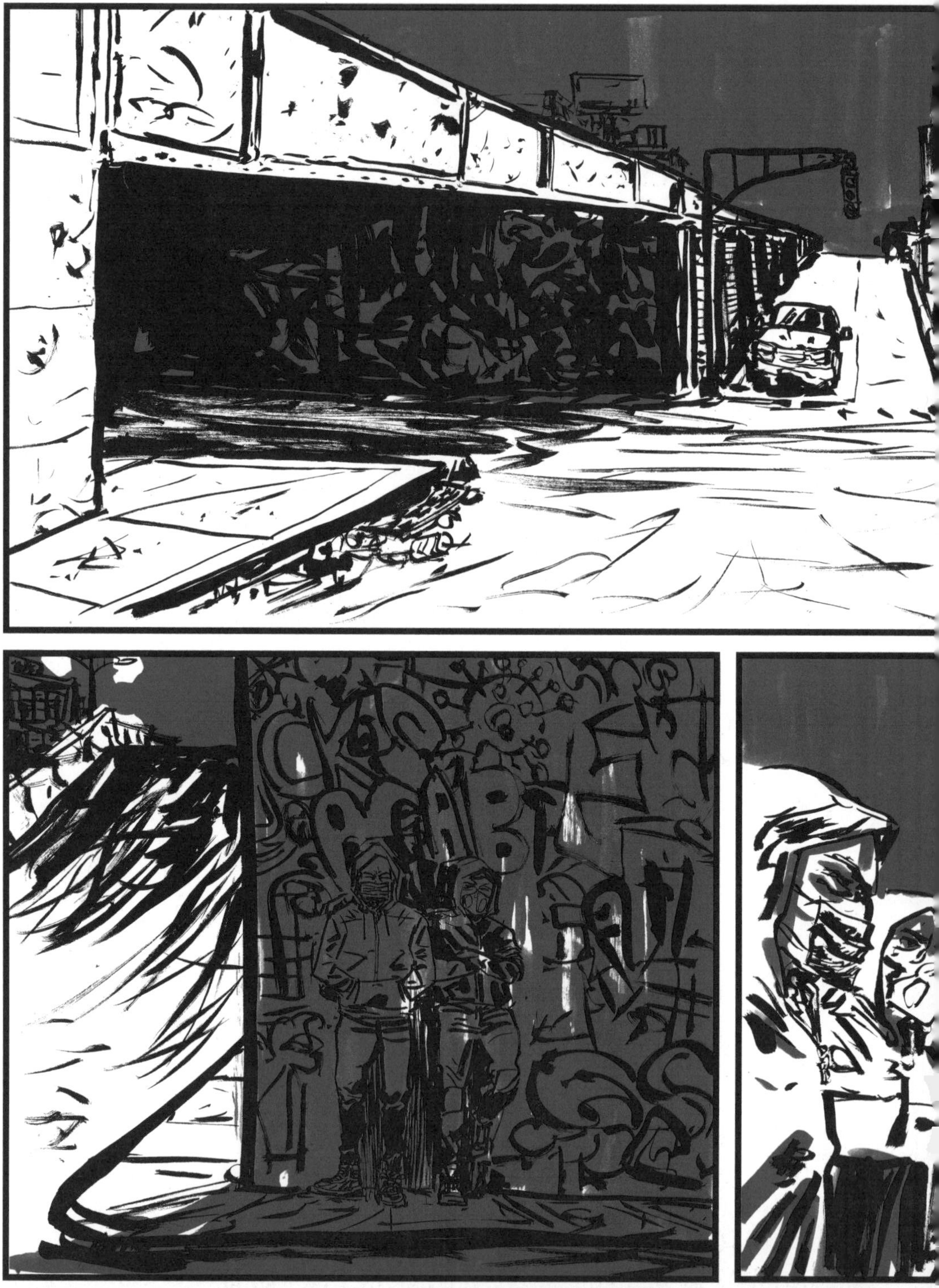

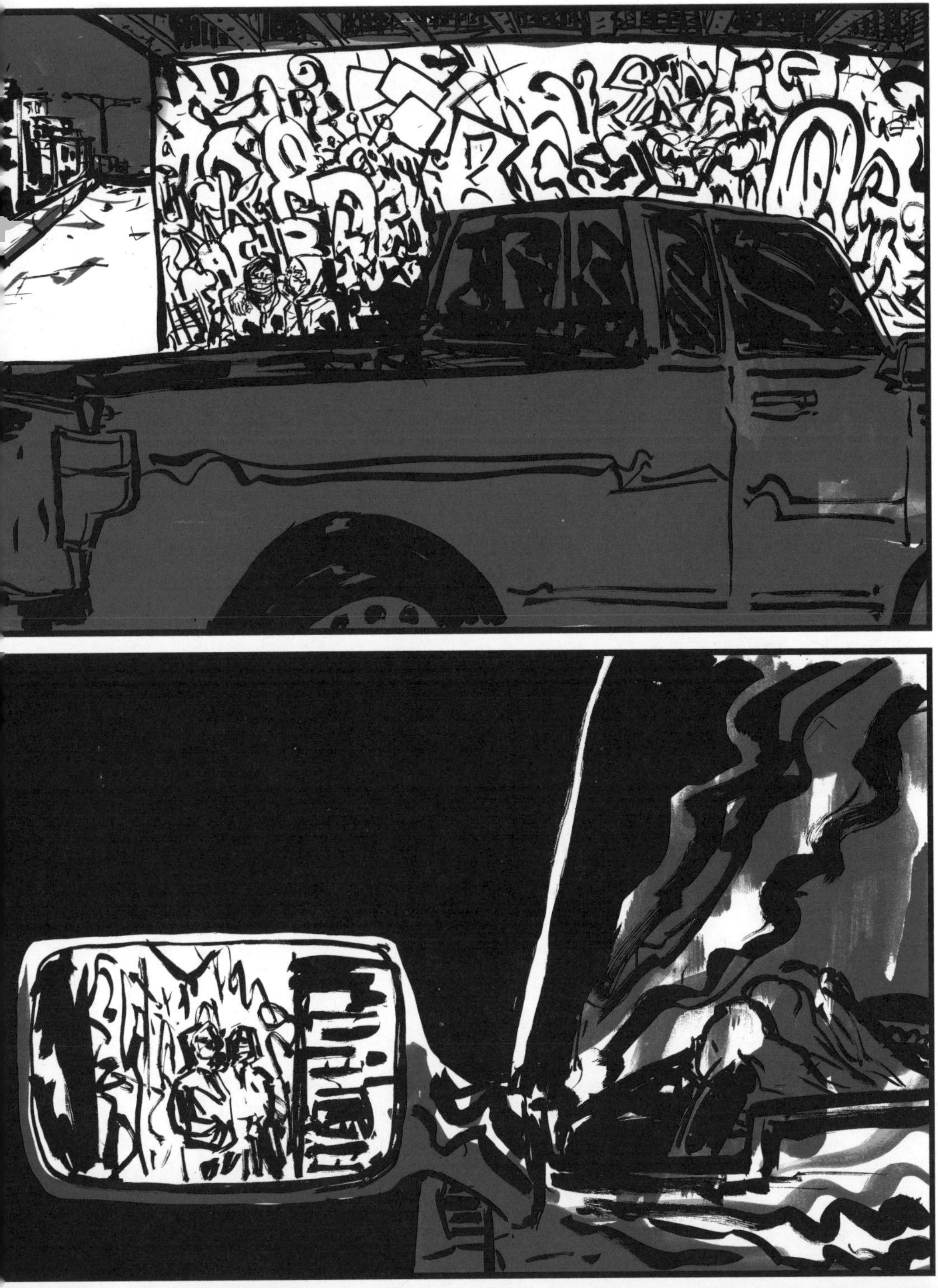

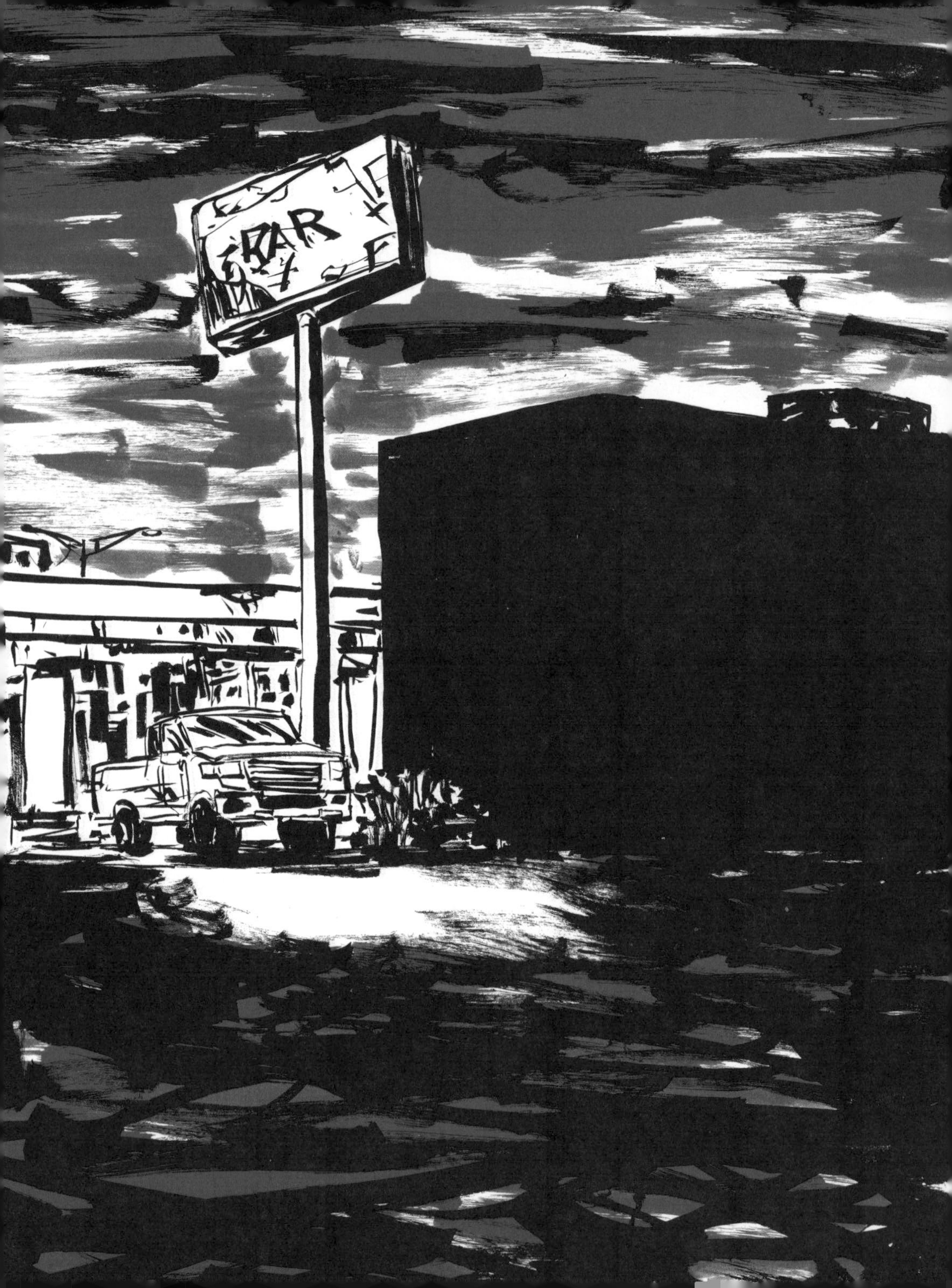

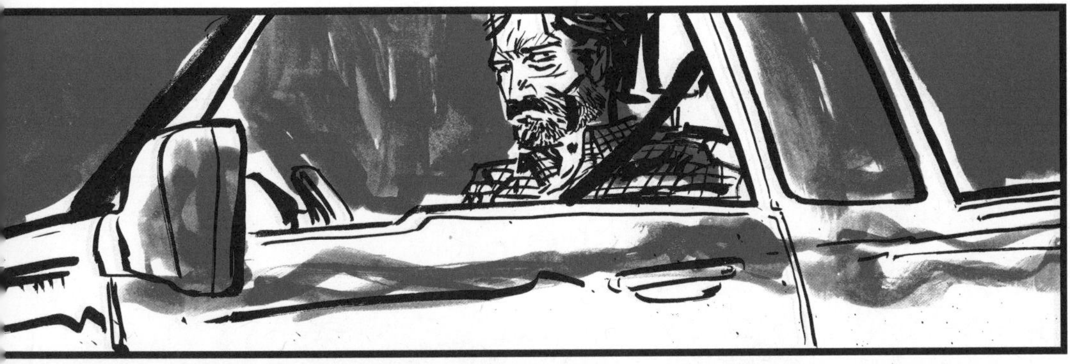
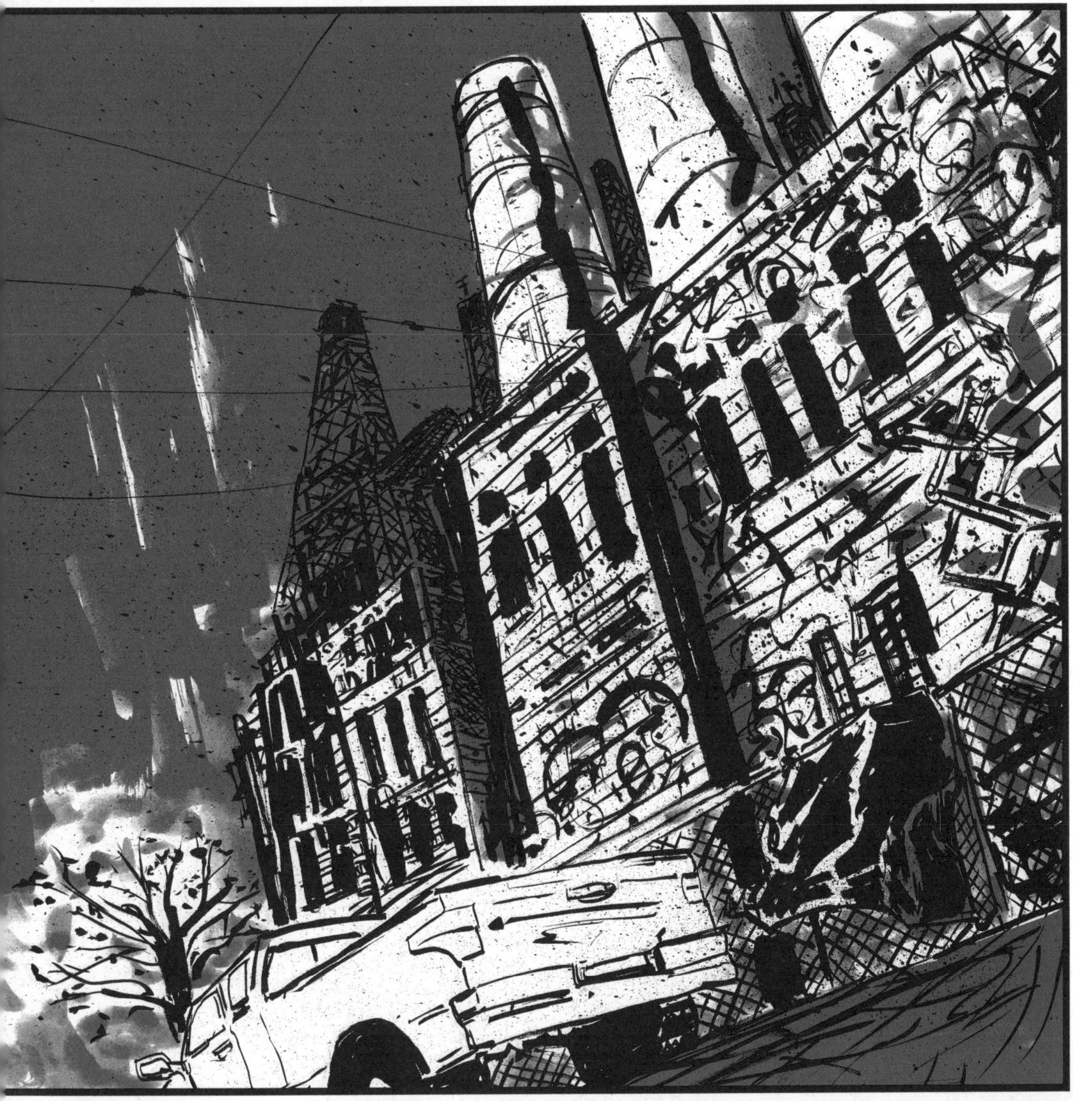

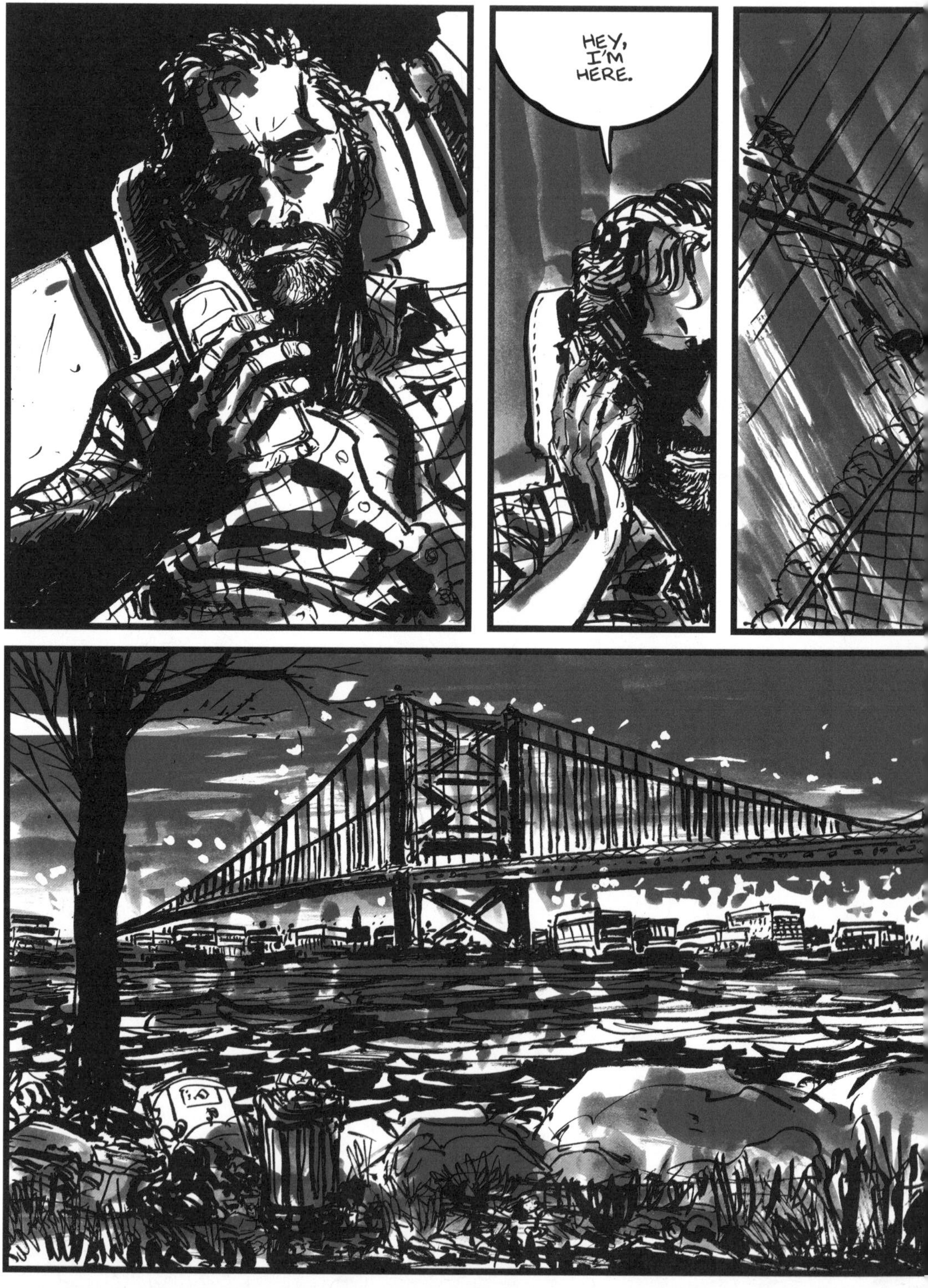
HEY, I'M HERE.

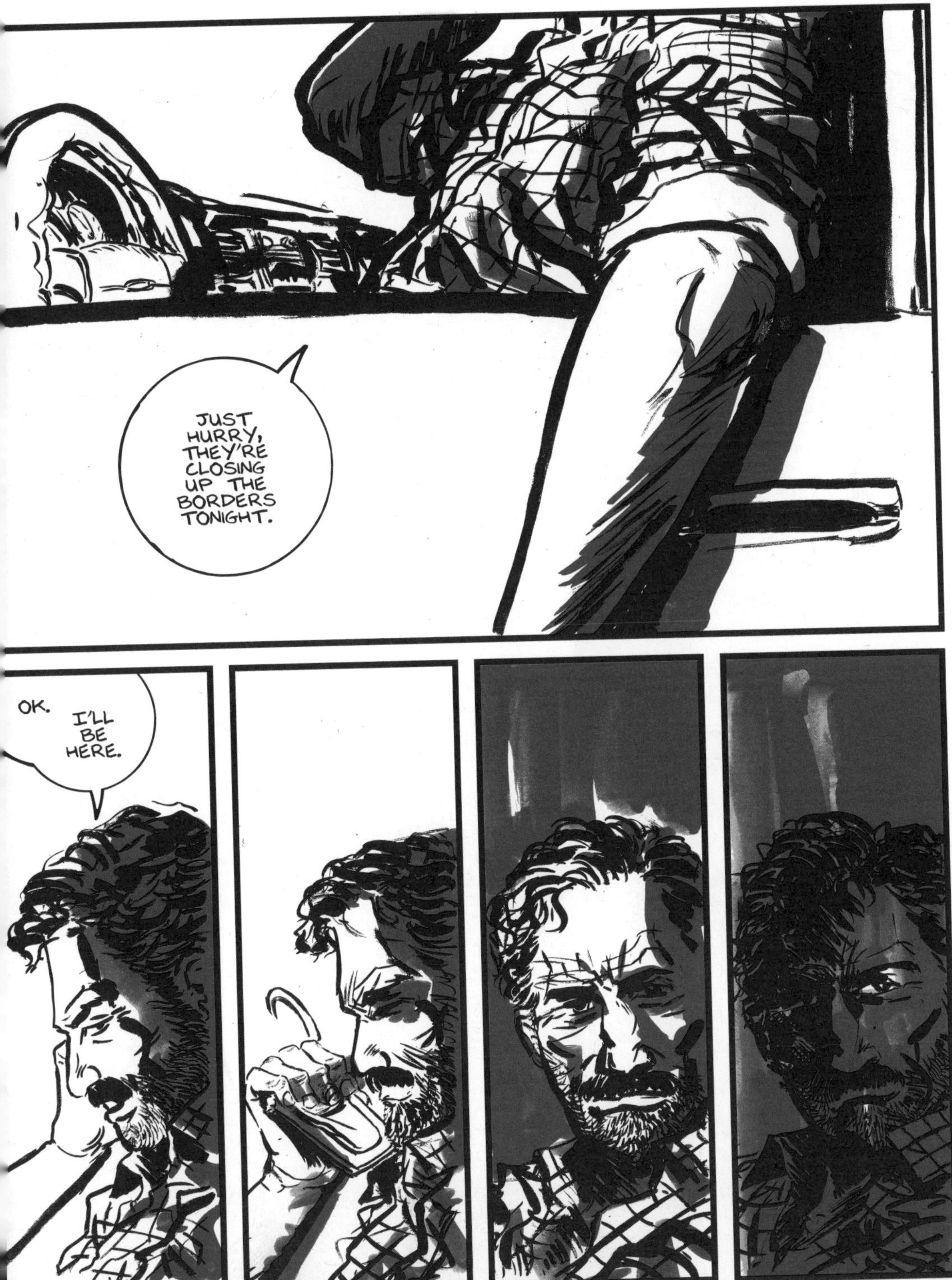
JUST HURRY, THEY'RE CLOSING UP THE BORDERS TONIGHT.
OK.
I'LL BE HERE.

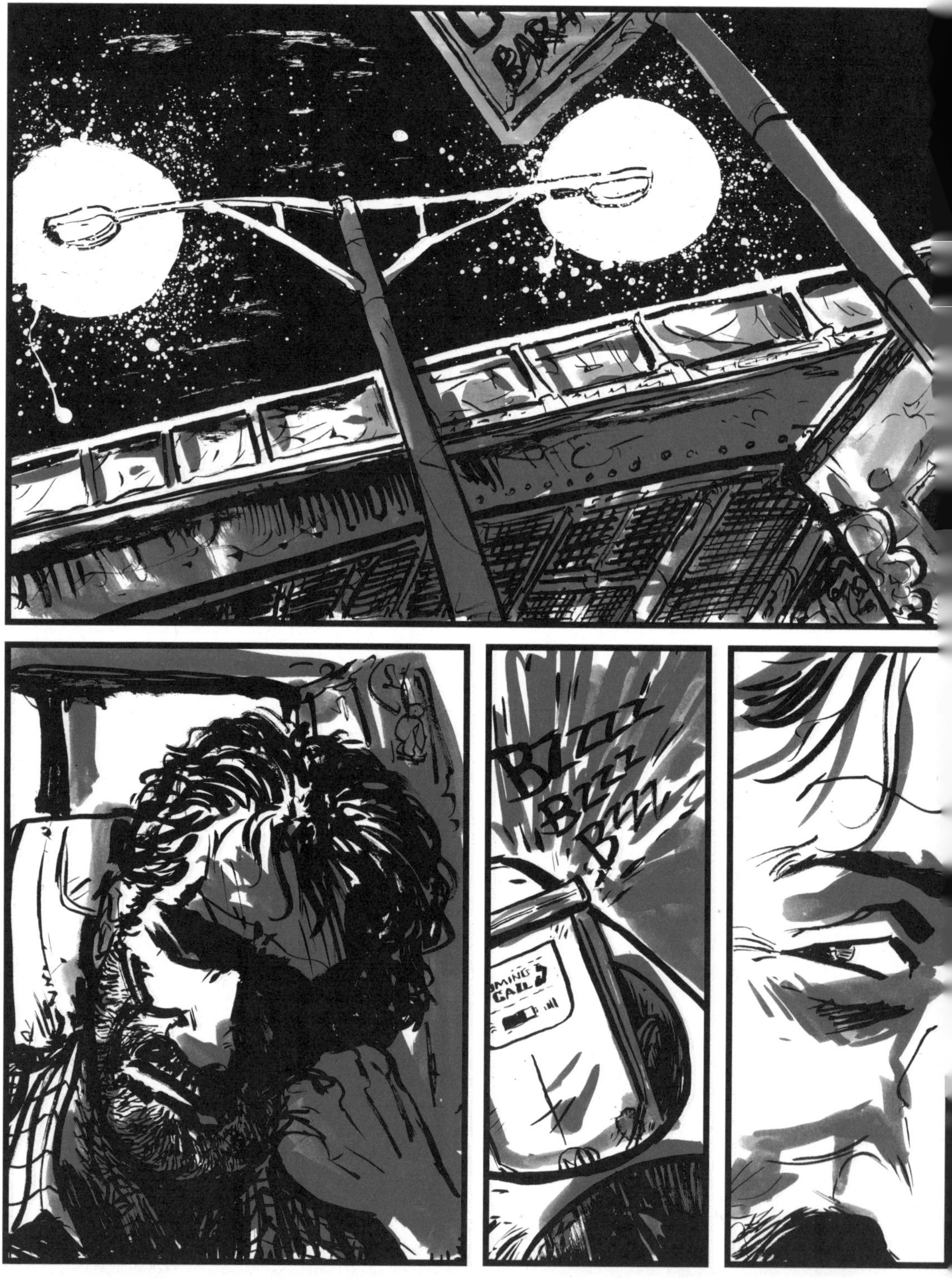
BZZZ
BZZZ
BZZZ
BZZZ
OMING
CALL

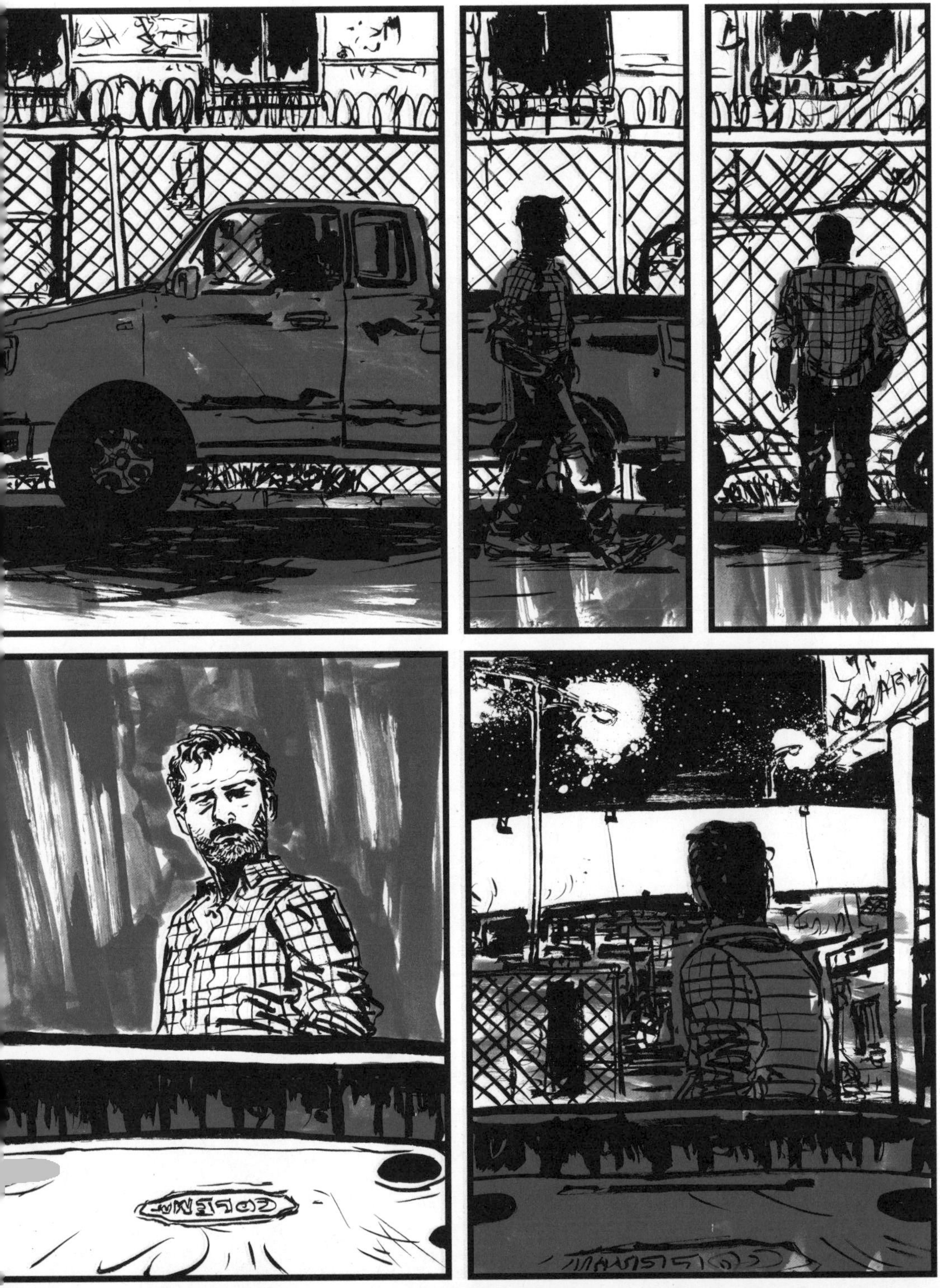

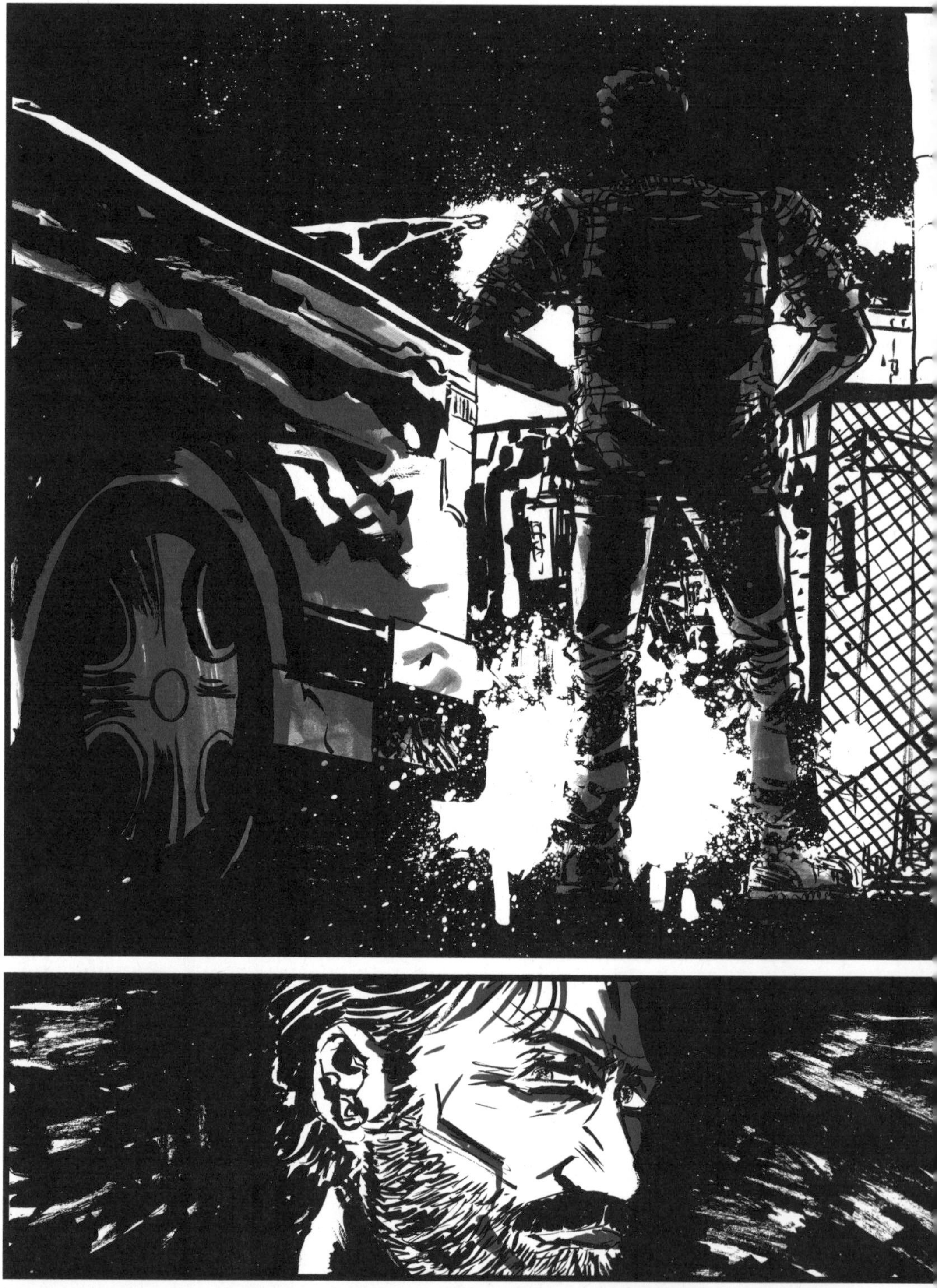

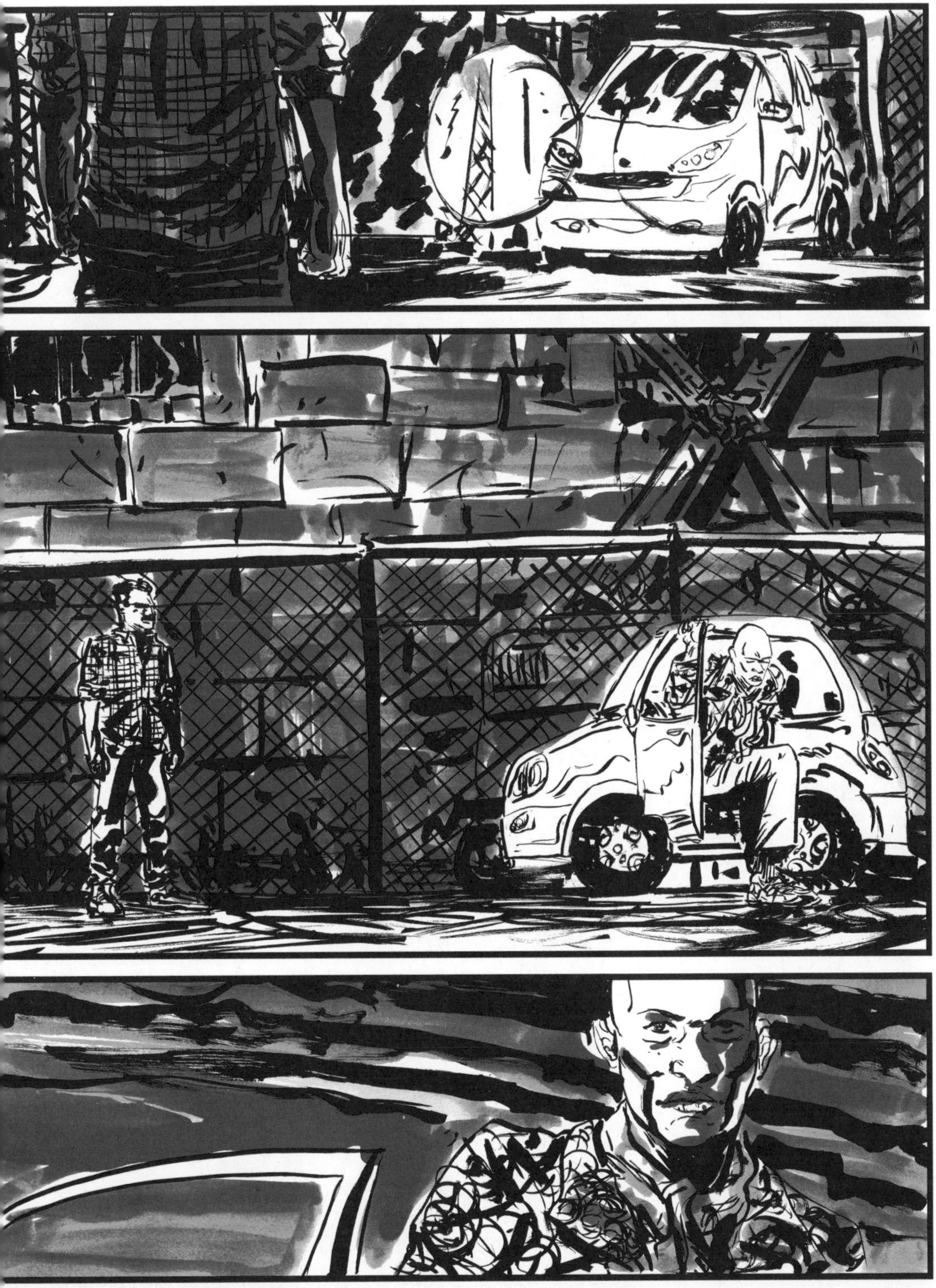

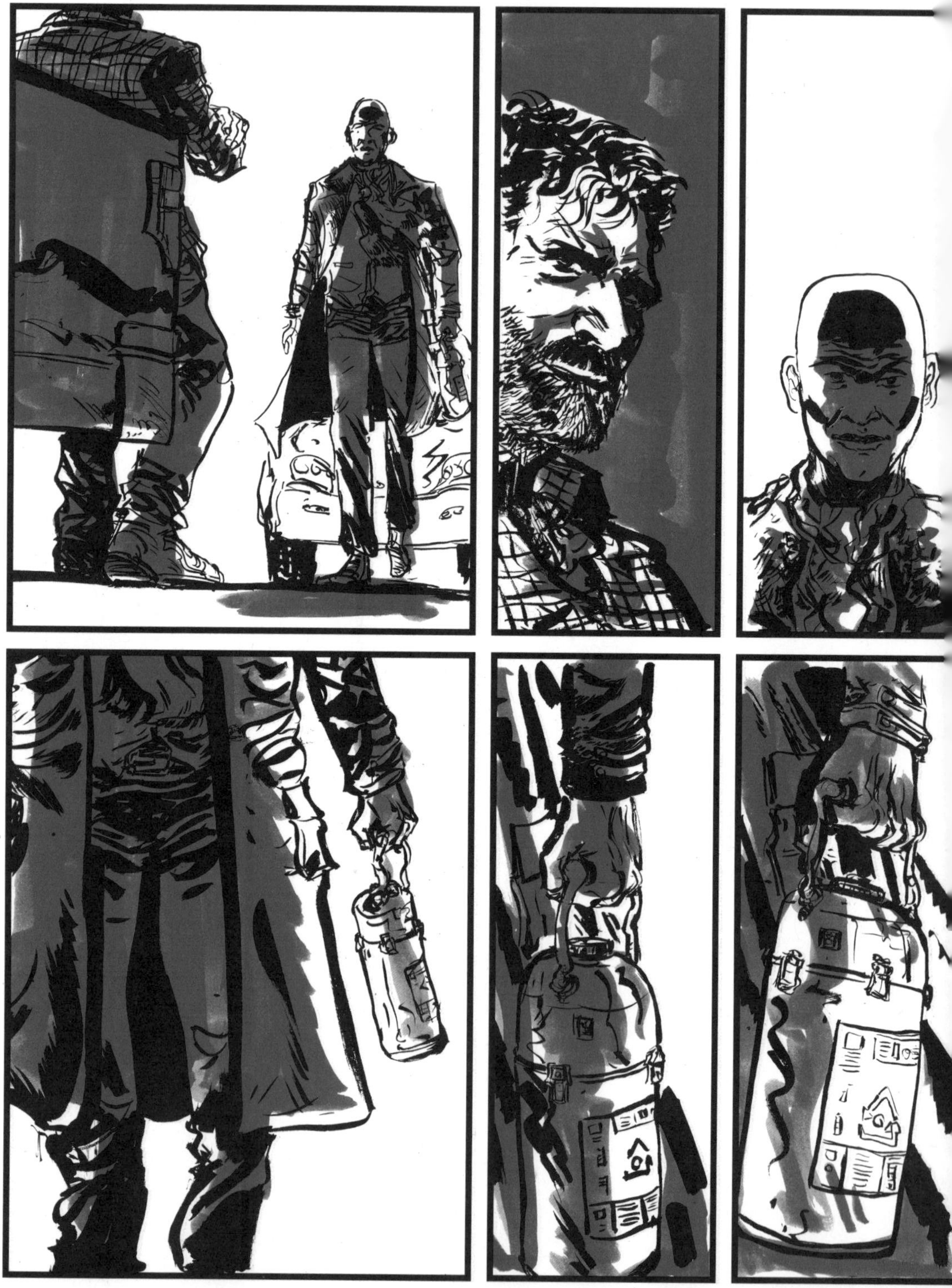

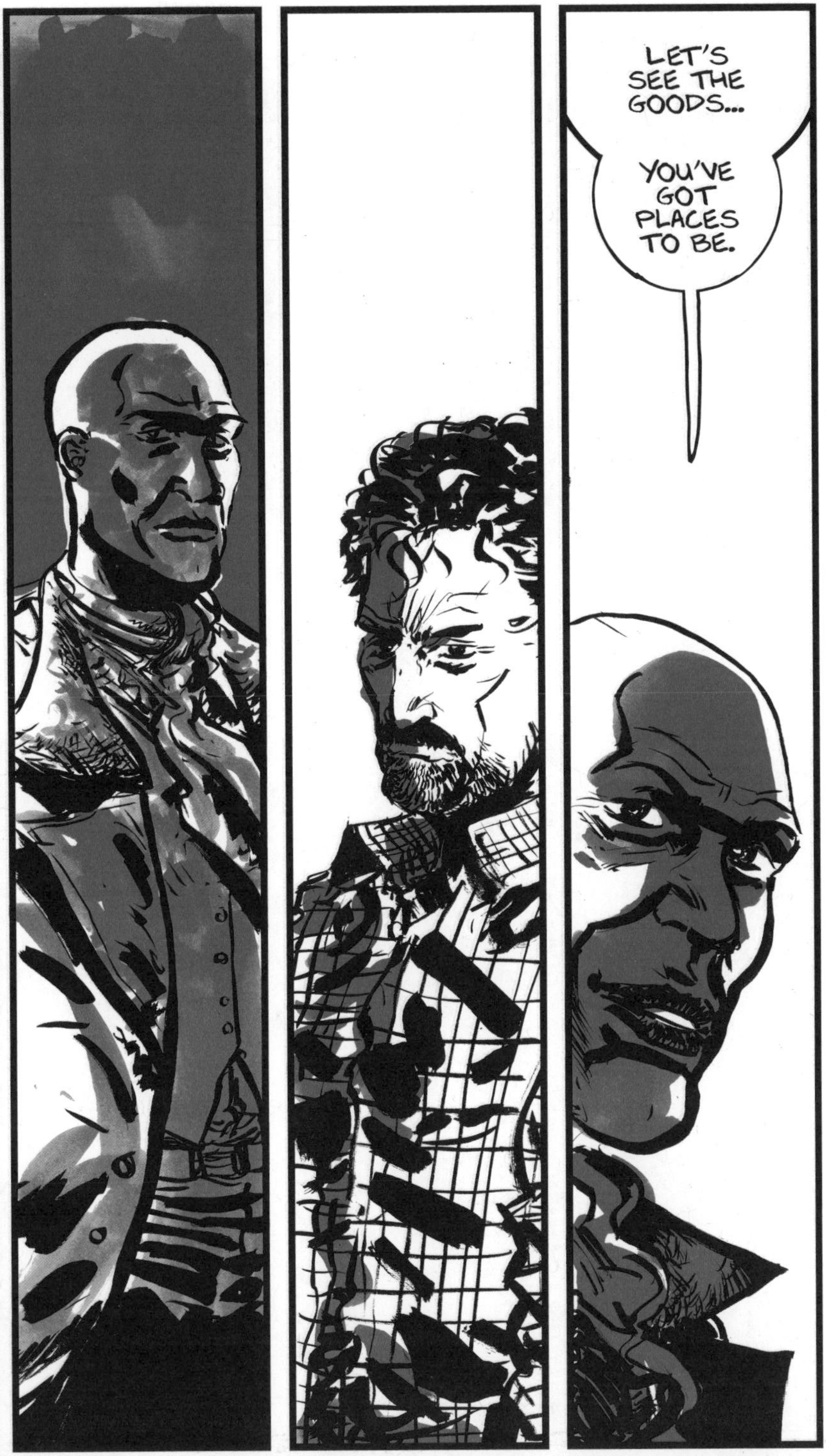
LET'S SEE THE GOODS...
YOU'VE GOT PLACES TO BE.

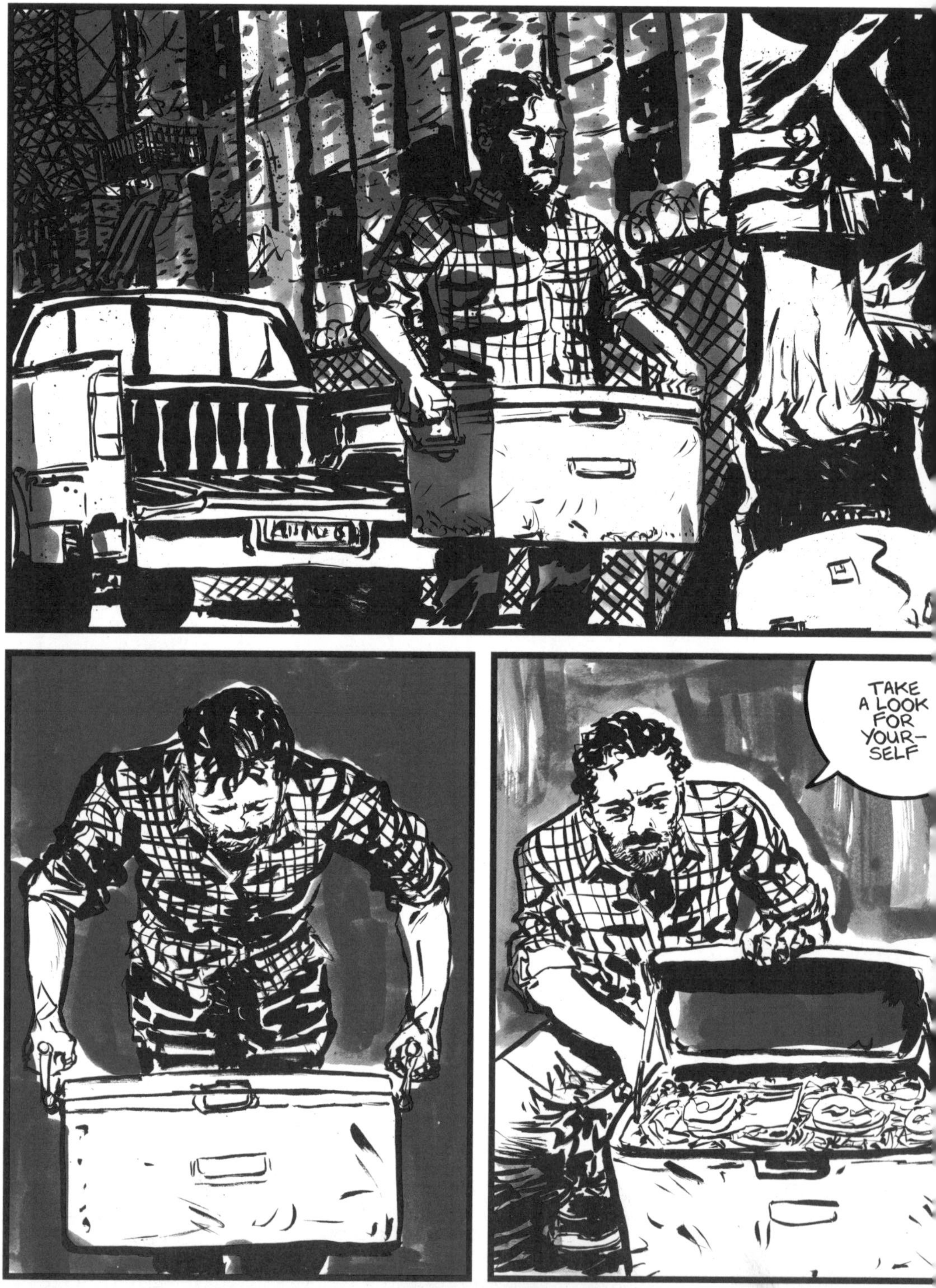
TAKE A LOOK FOR YOUR-SELF

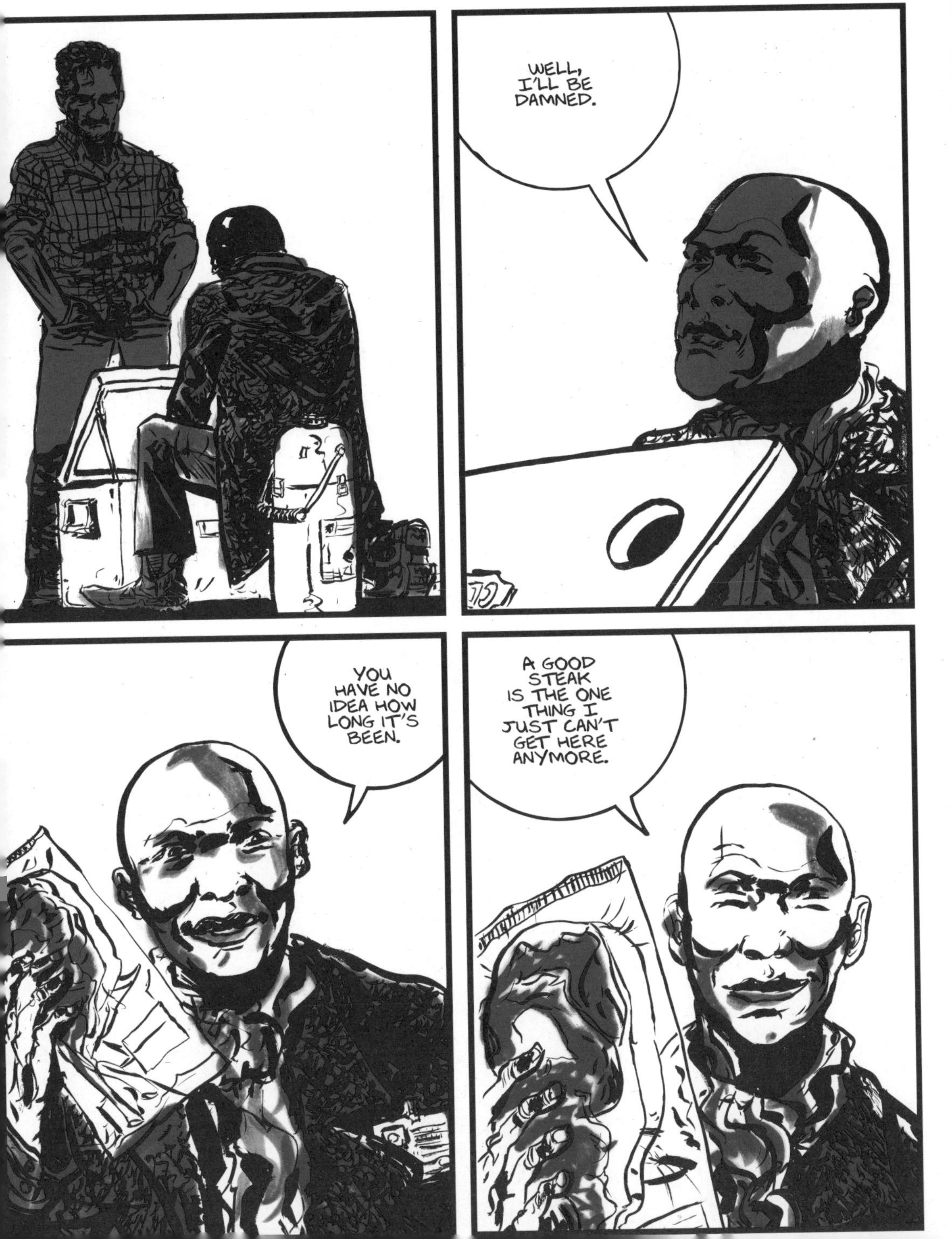
WELL, I'LL BE DAMNED.
YOU HAVE NO IDEA HOW LONG IT'S BEEN.
A GOOD STEAK IS THE ONE THING I JUST CAN'T GET HERE ANYMORE.

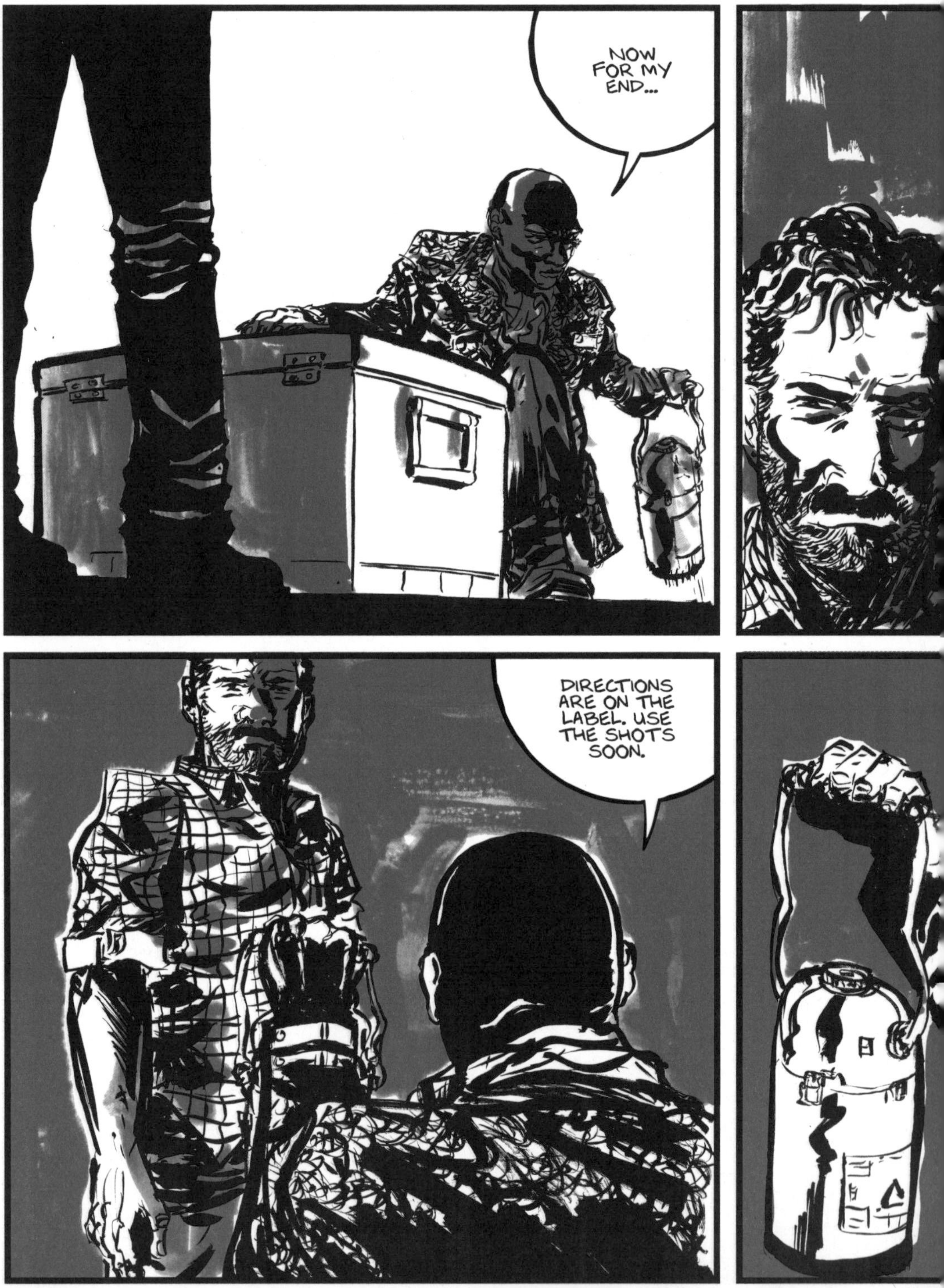
NOW FOR MY END...
DIRECTIONS ARE ON THE LABEL. USE THE SHOTS SOON.

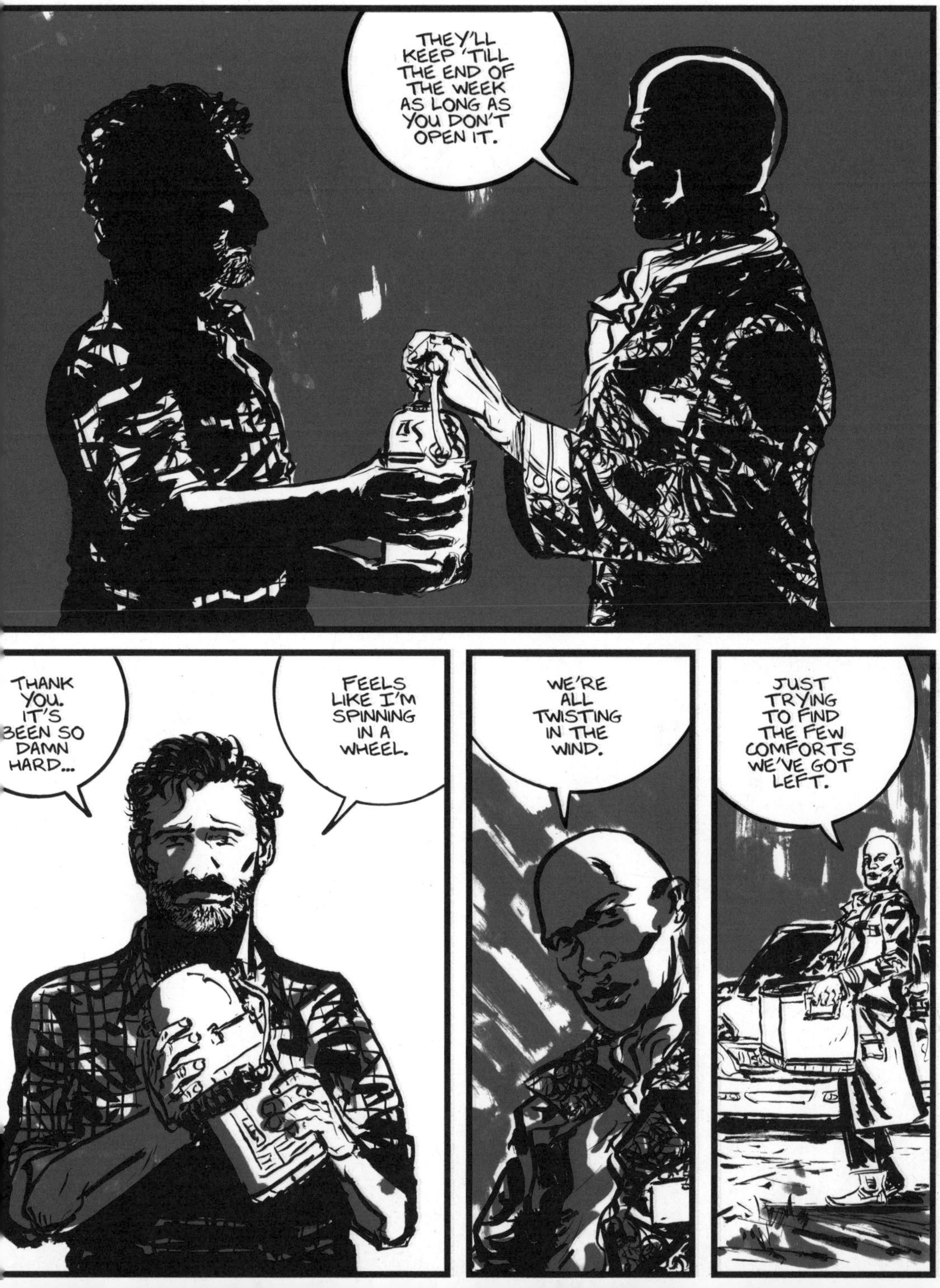
THEY'LL KEEP 'TILL THE END OF THE WEEK AS LONG AS YOU DON'T OPEN IT.
THANK YOU. IT'S BEEN SO DAMN HARD...
FEELS LIKE I'M SPINNING IN A WHEEL.
WE'RE ALL TWISTING IN THE WIND.
JUST TRYING TO FIND THE FEW COMFORTS WE'VE GOT LEFT.

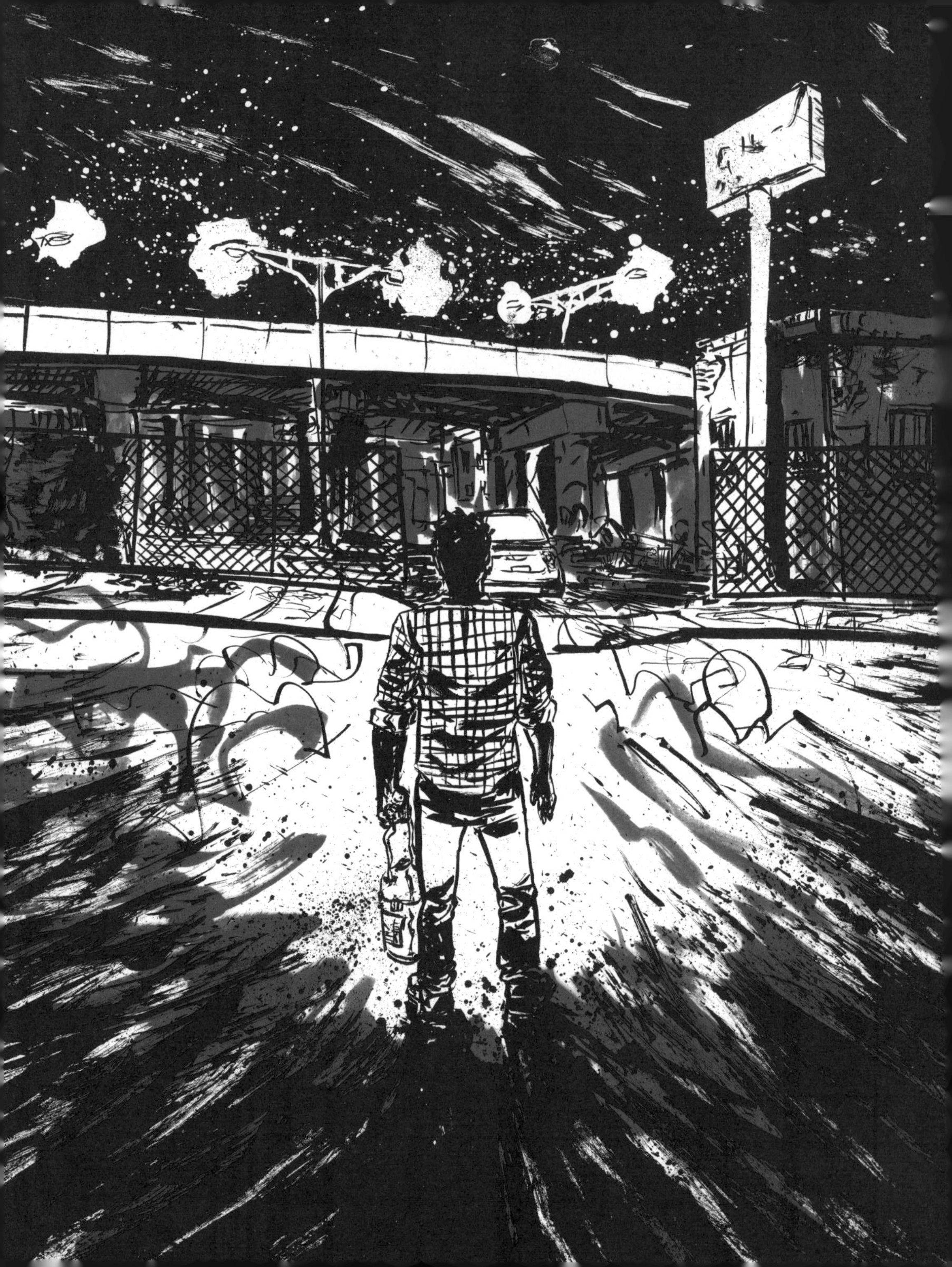

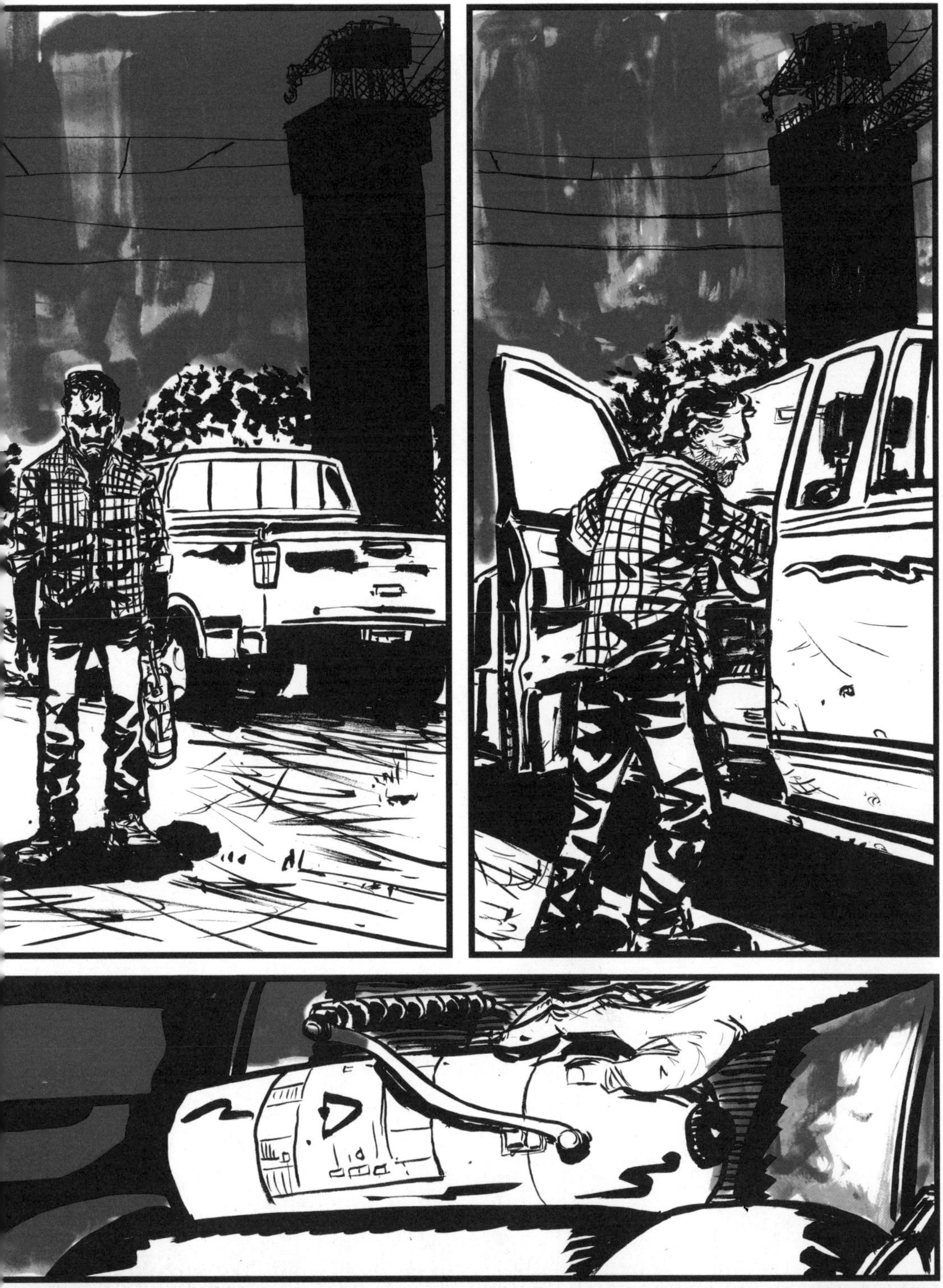

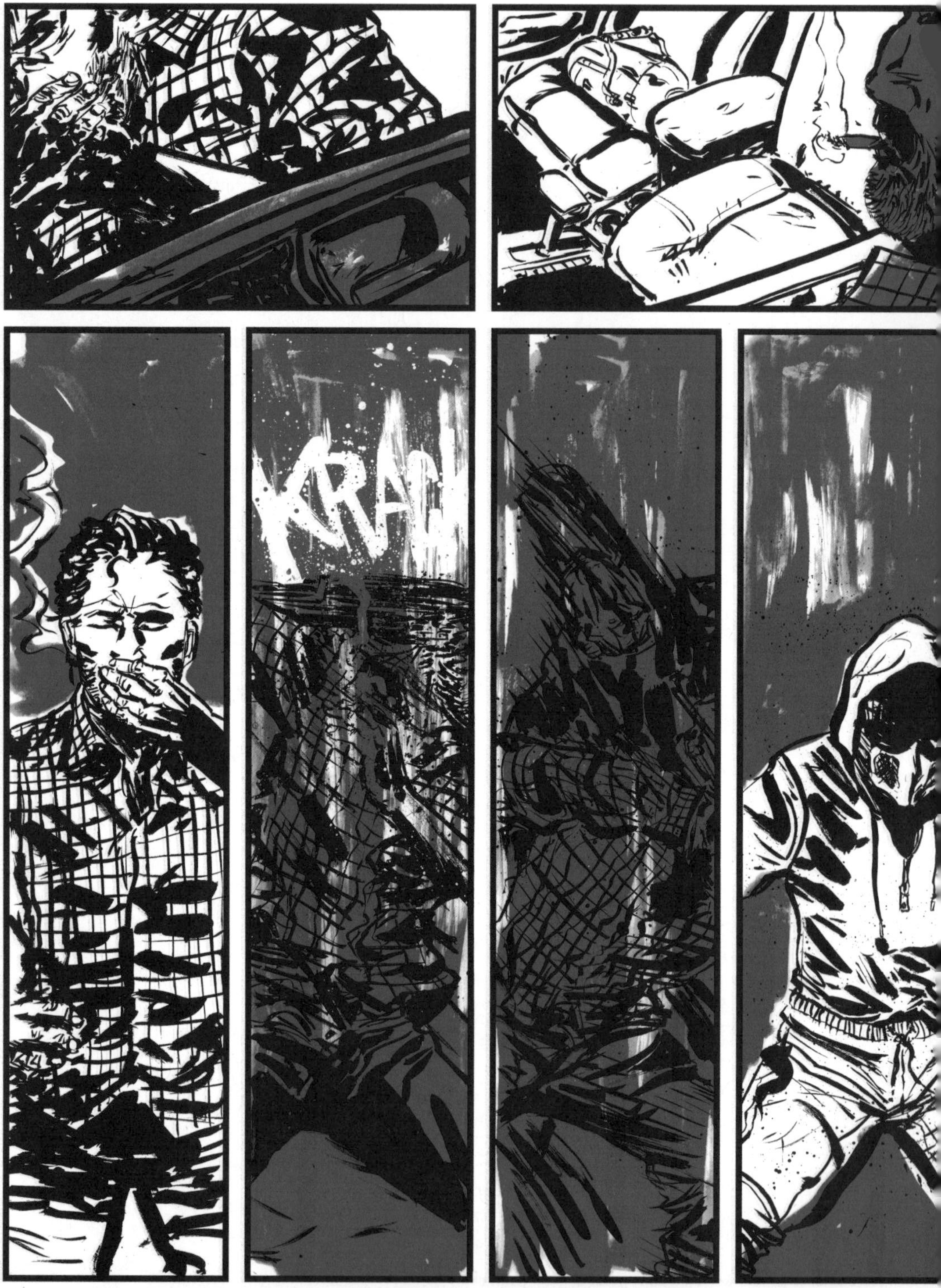
KRAC

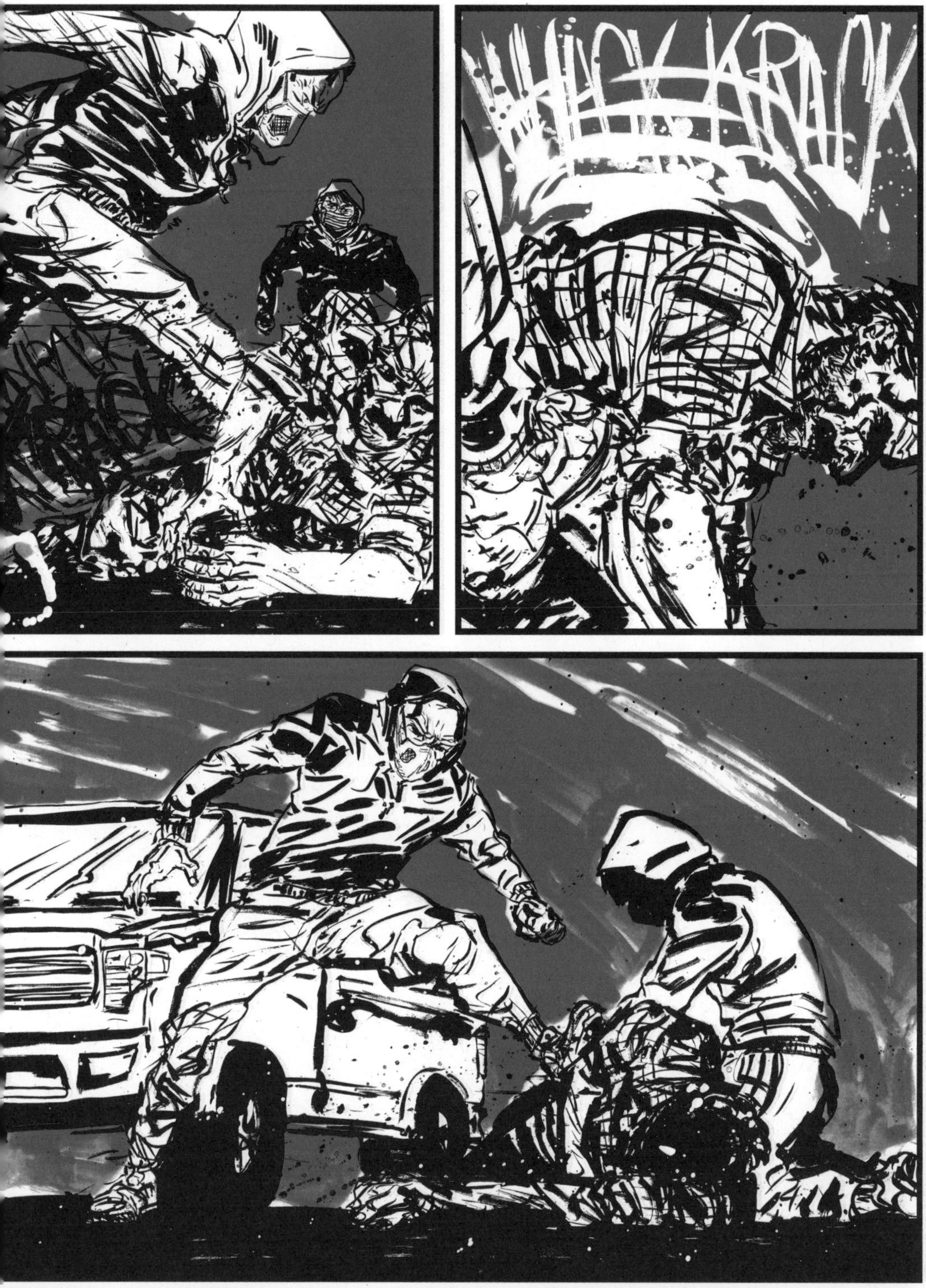

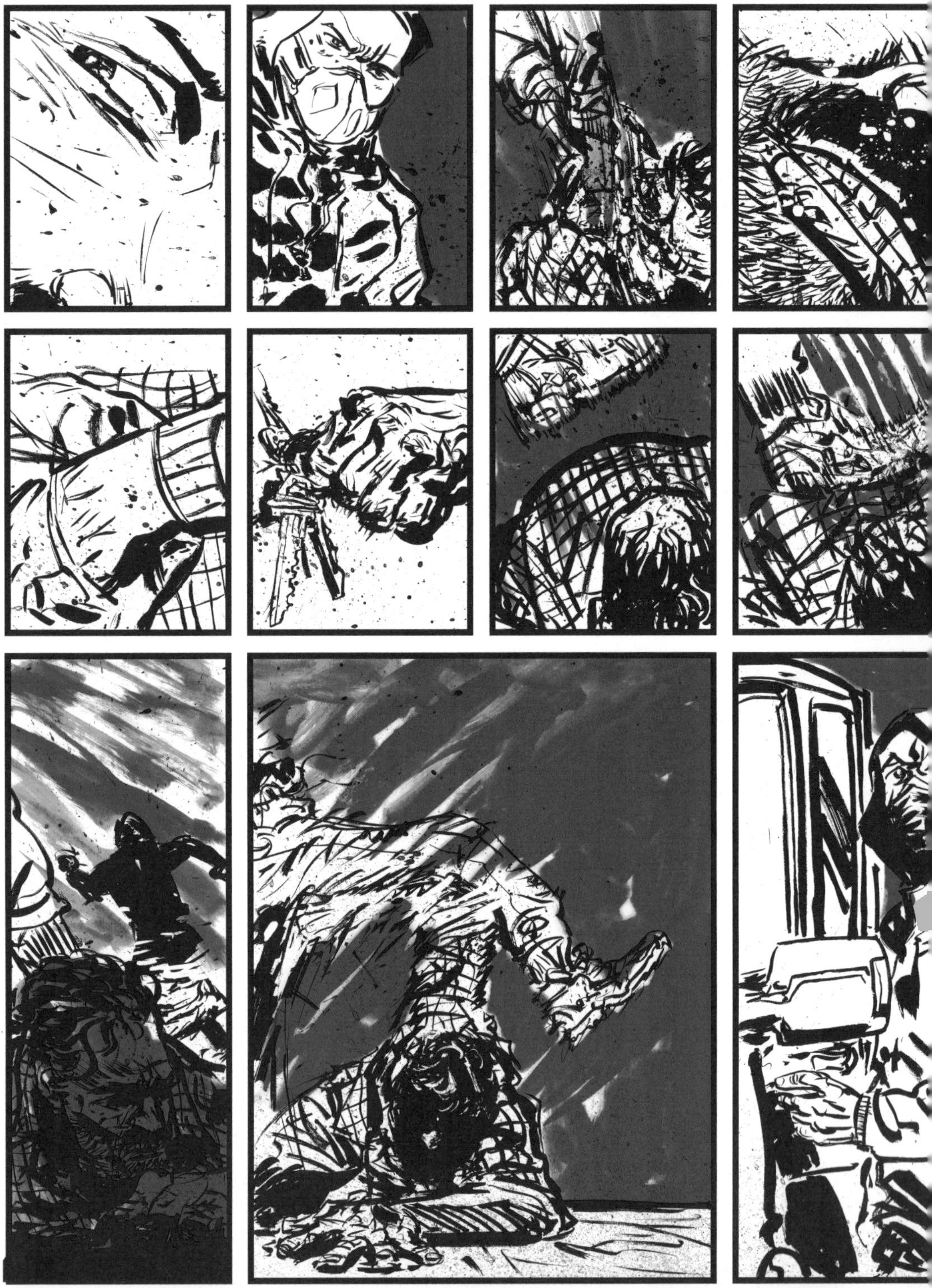

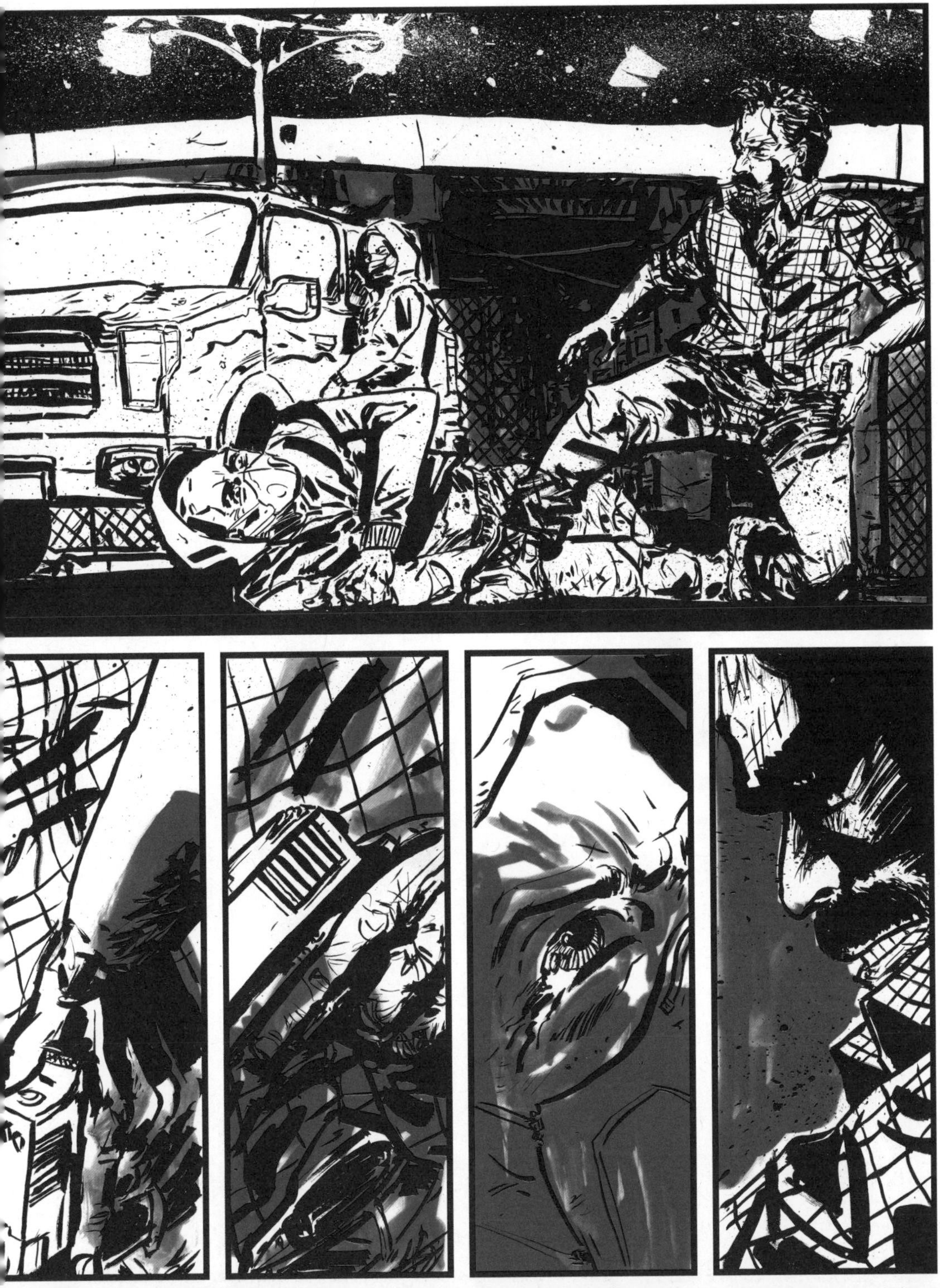

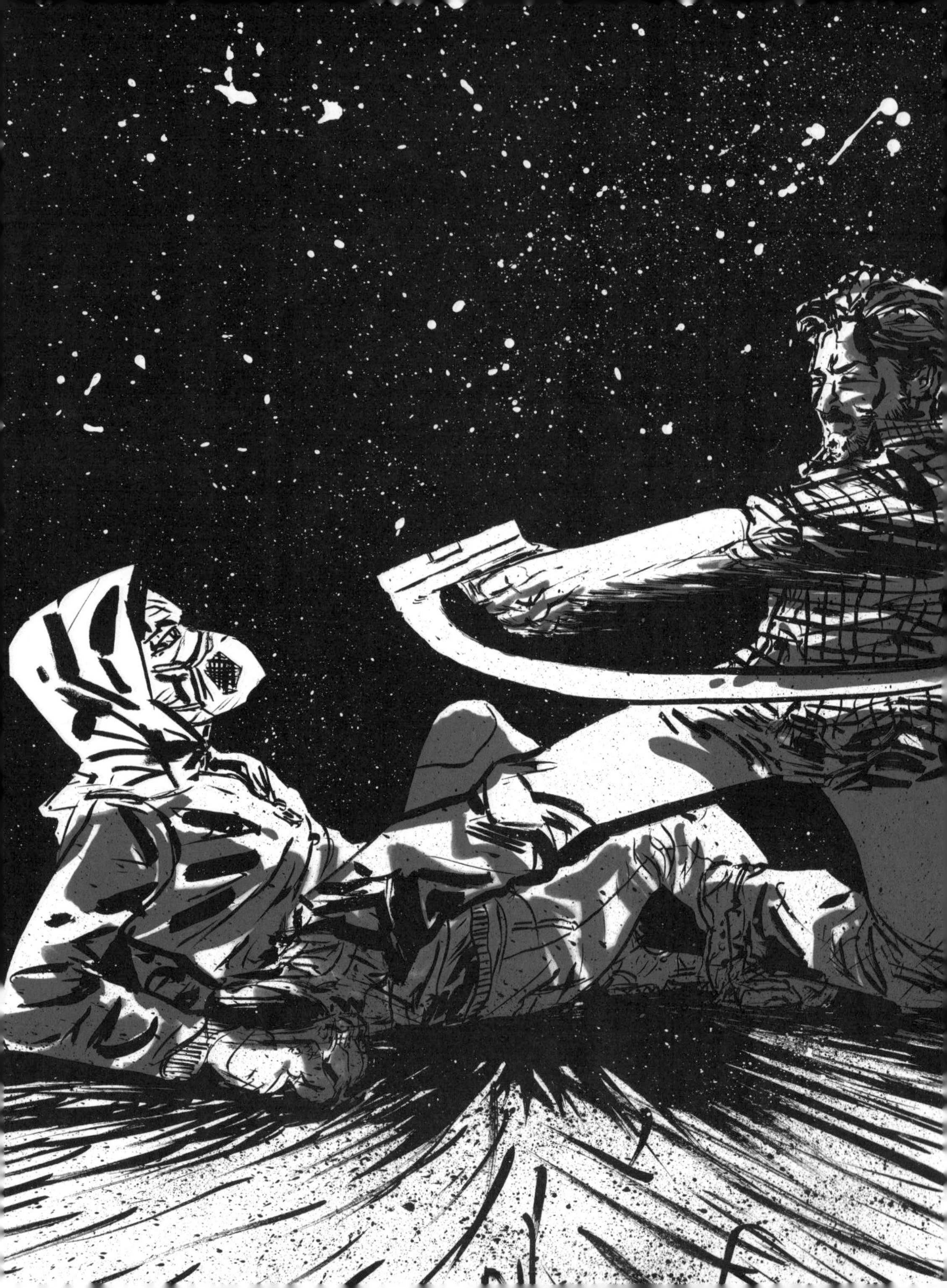

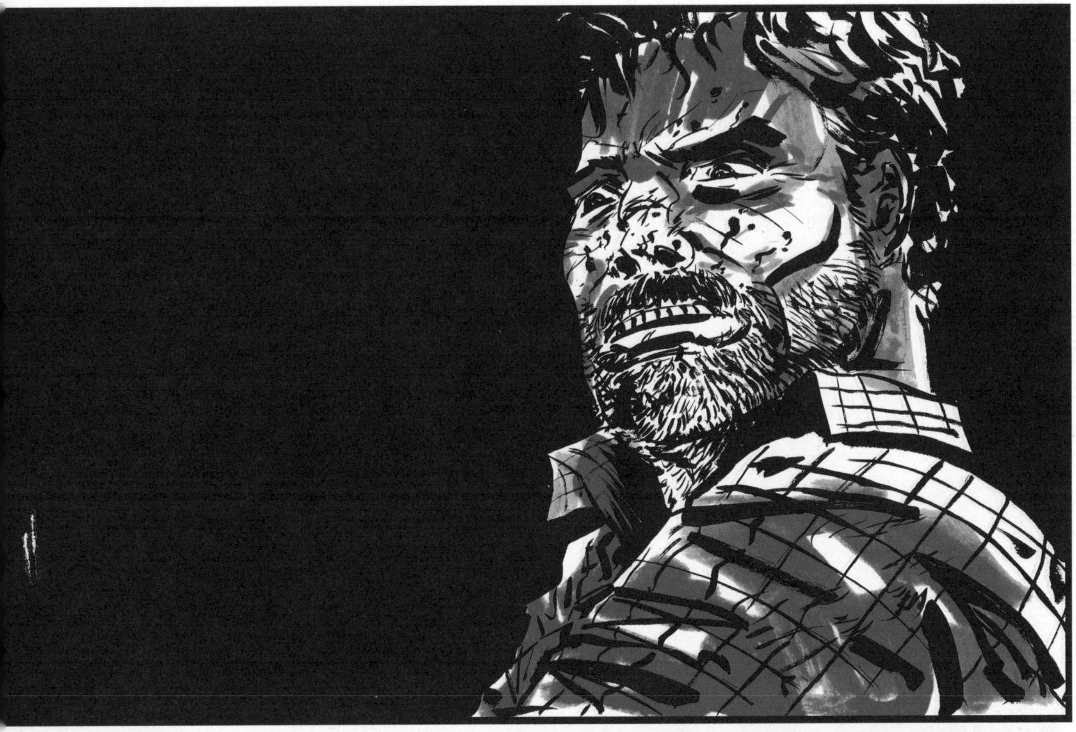
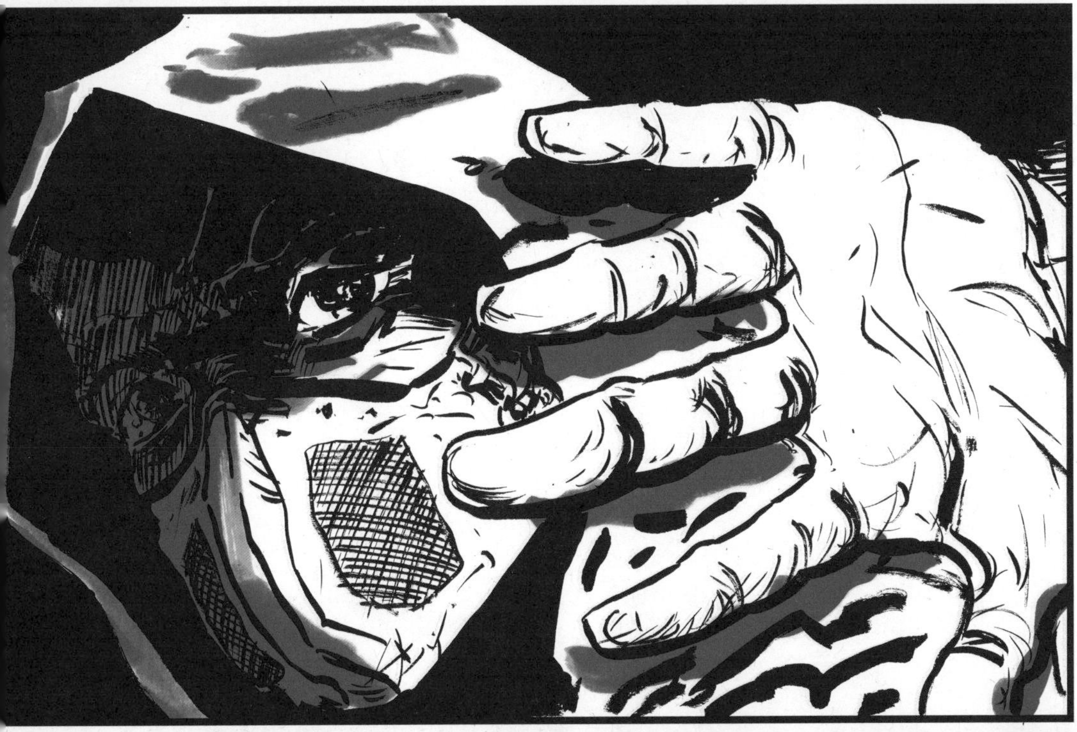

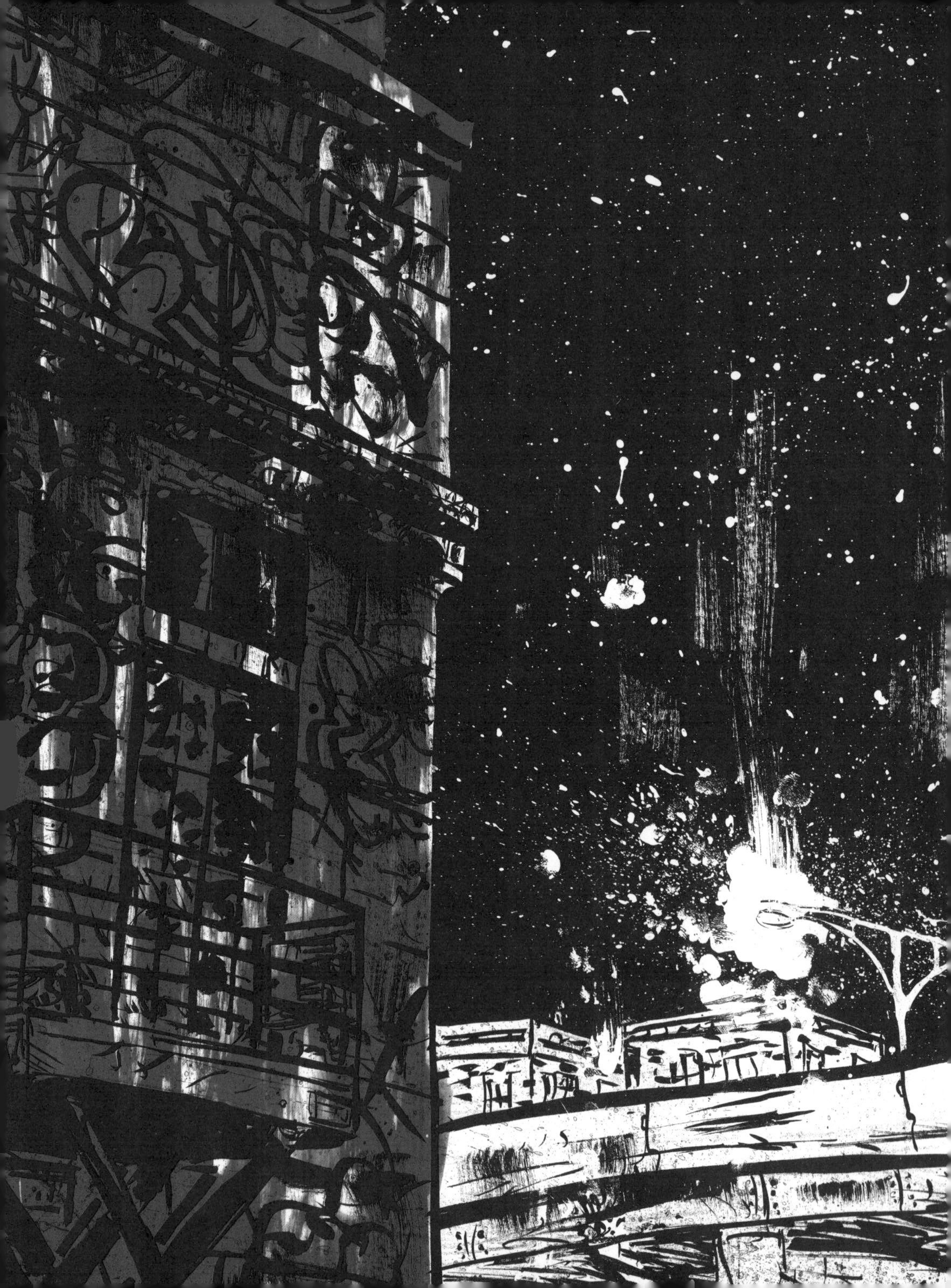

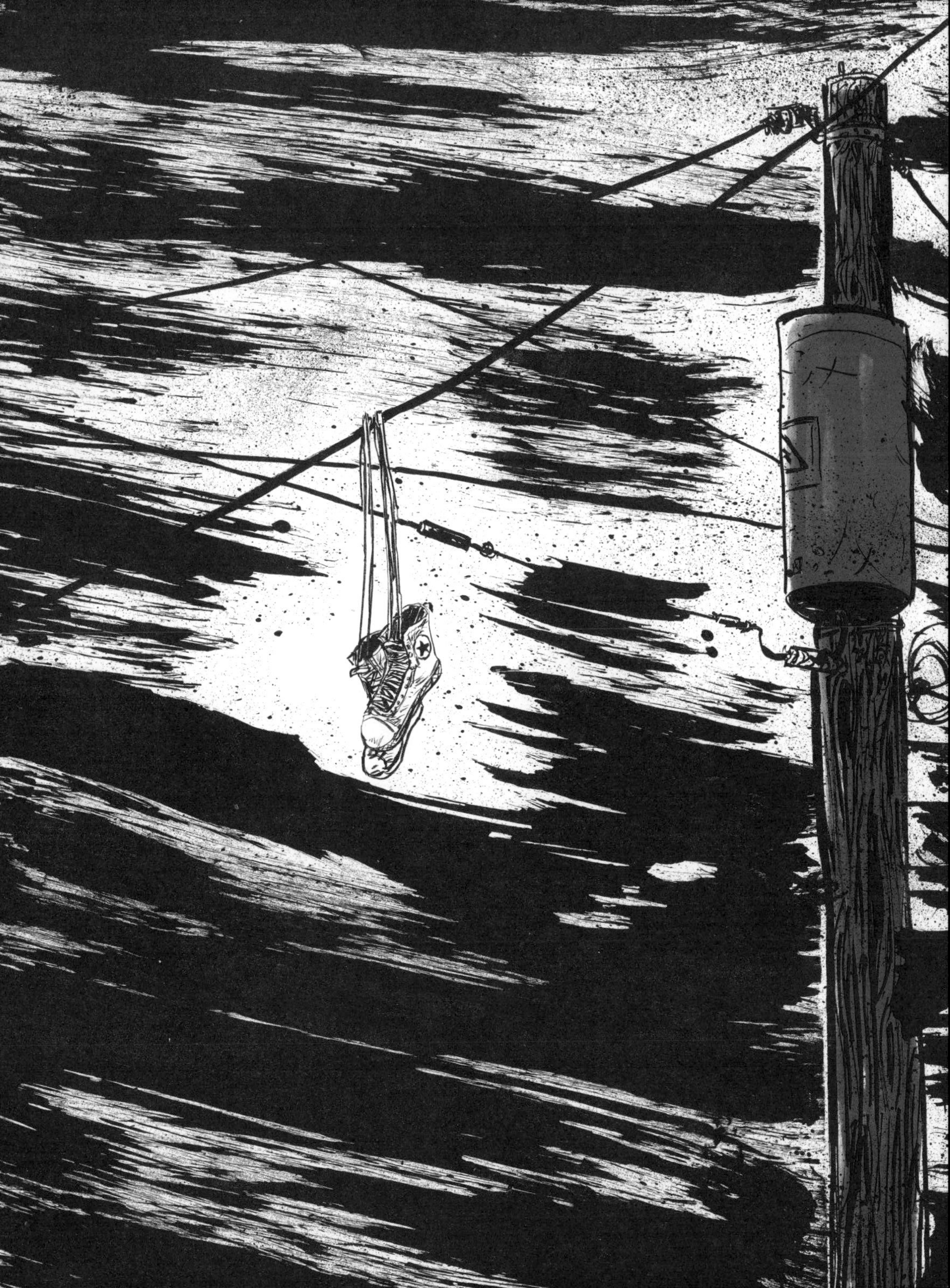

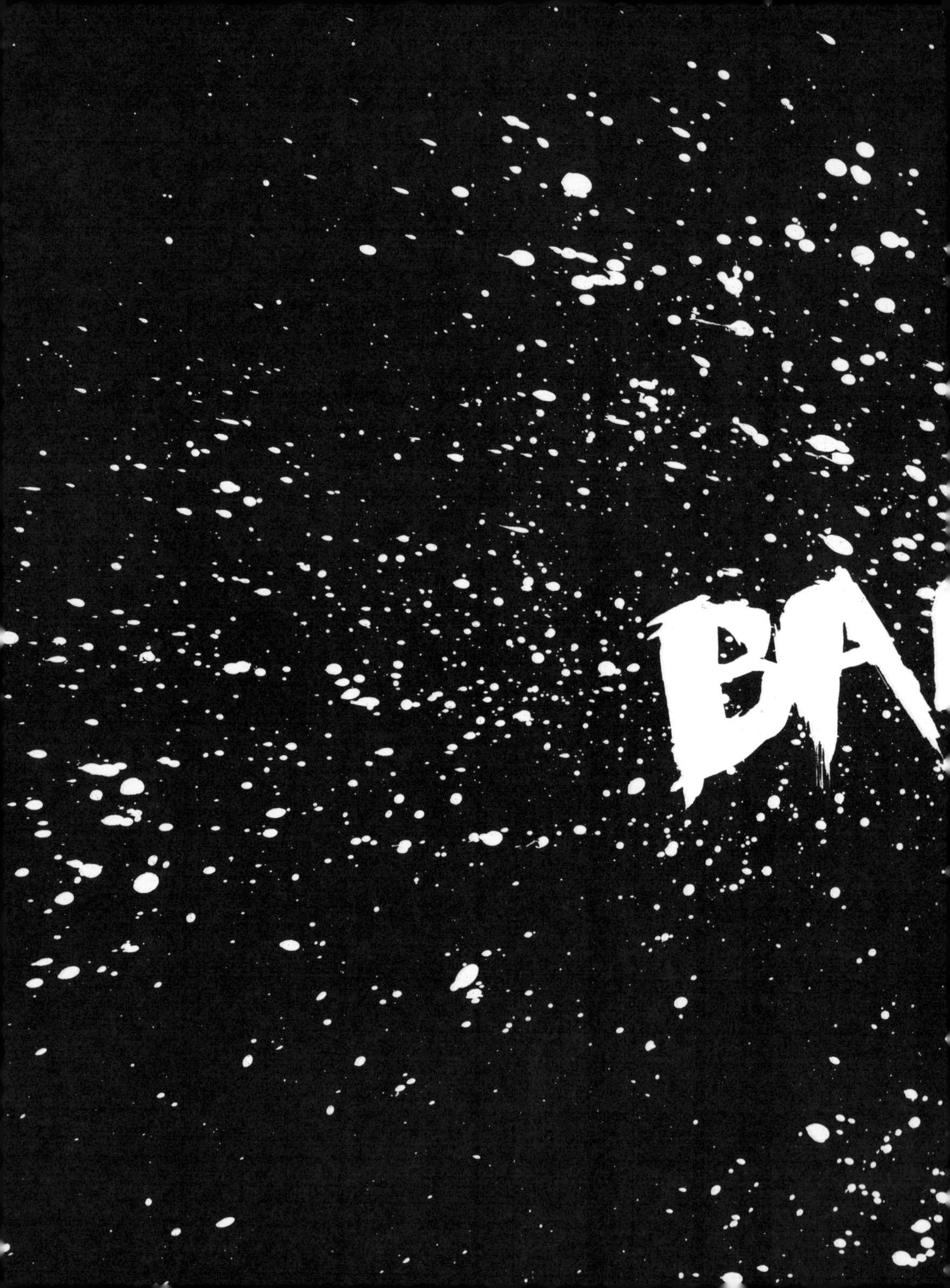
BA

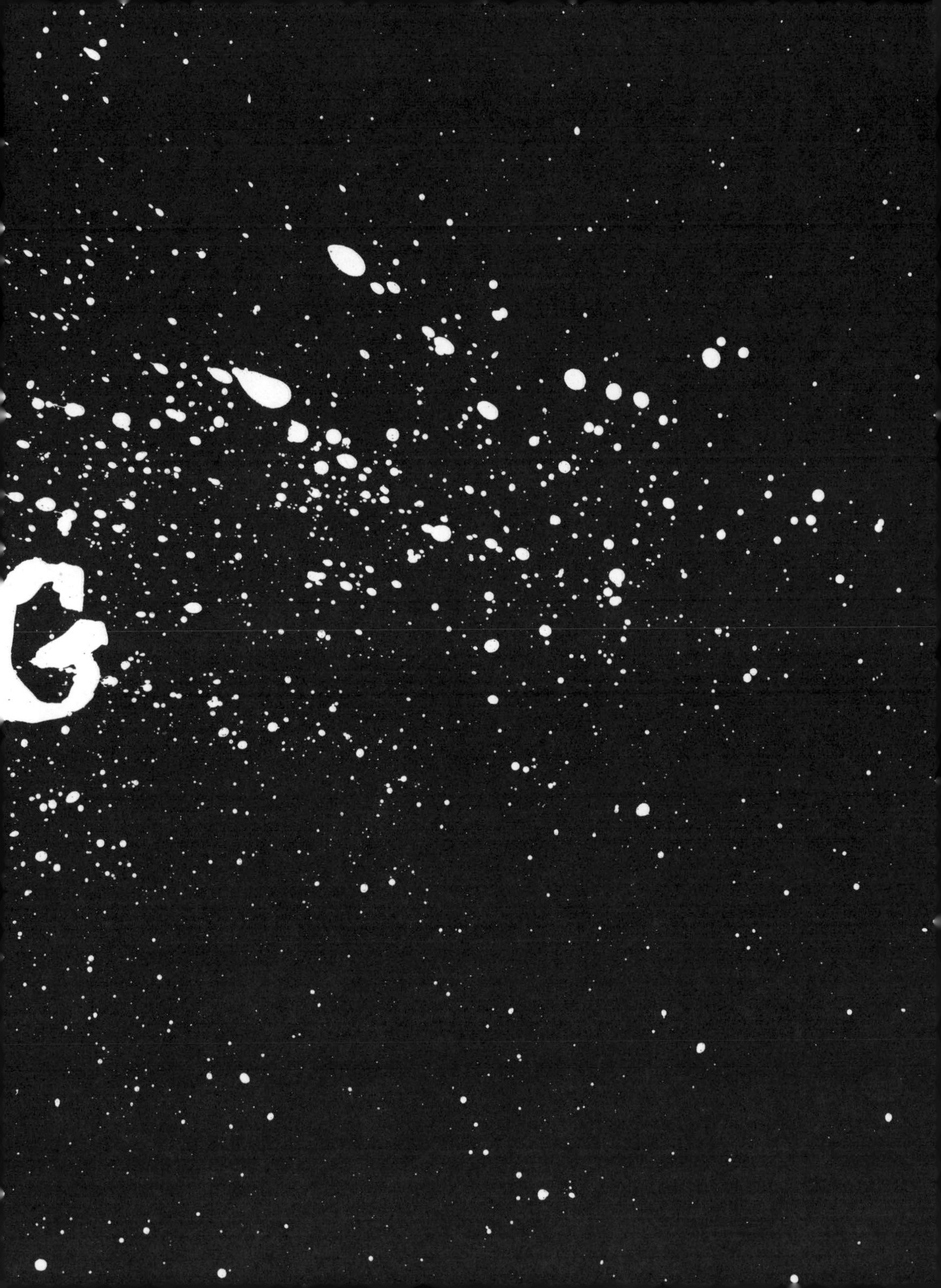
G

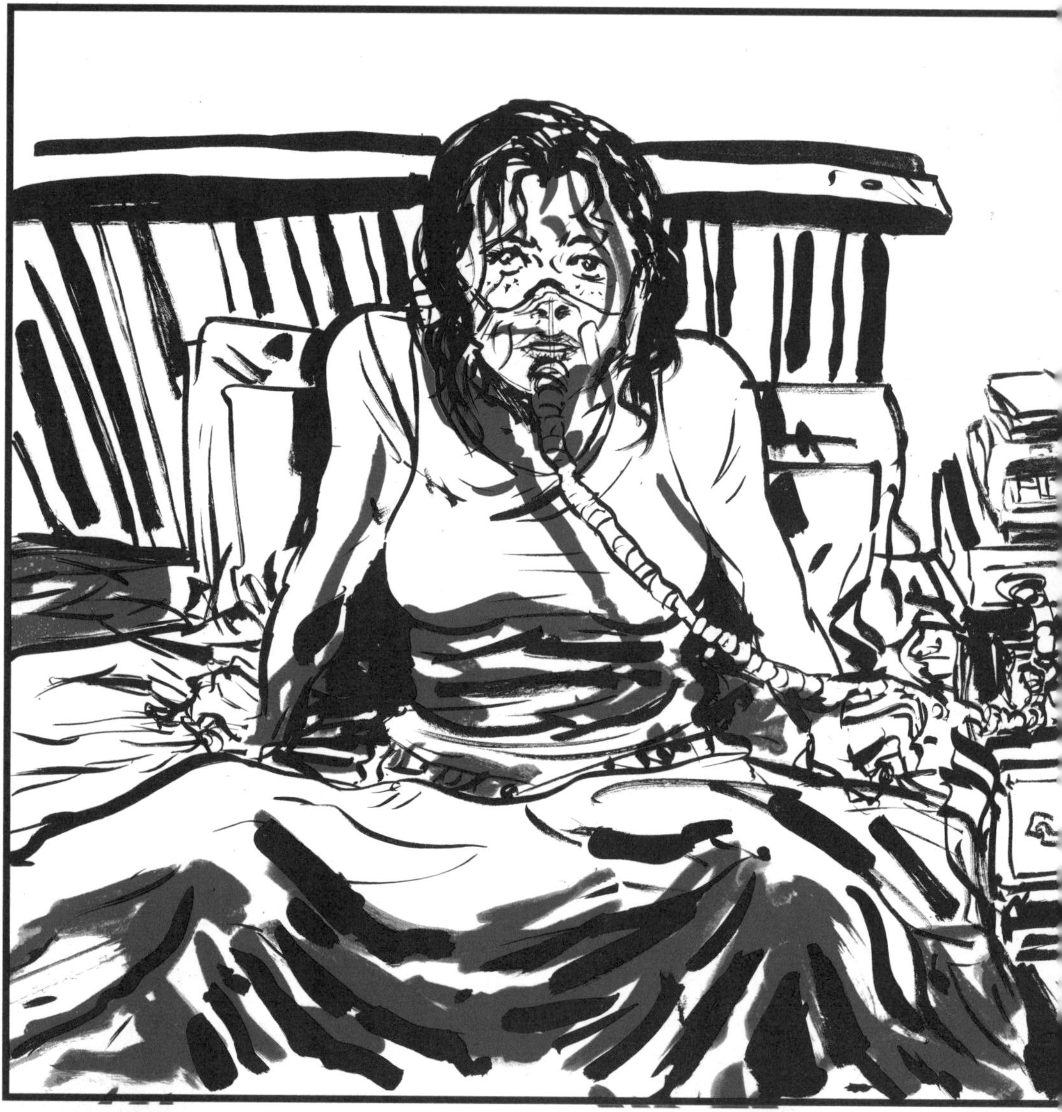
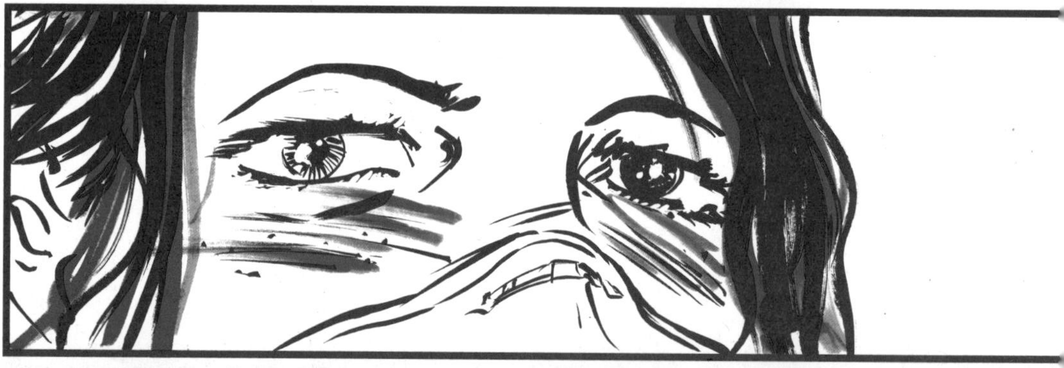

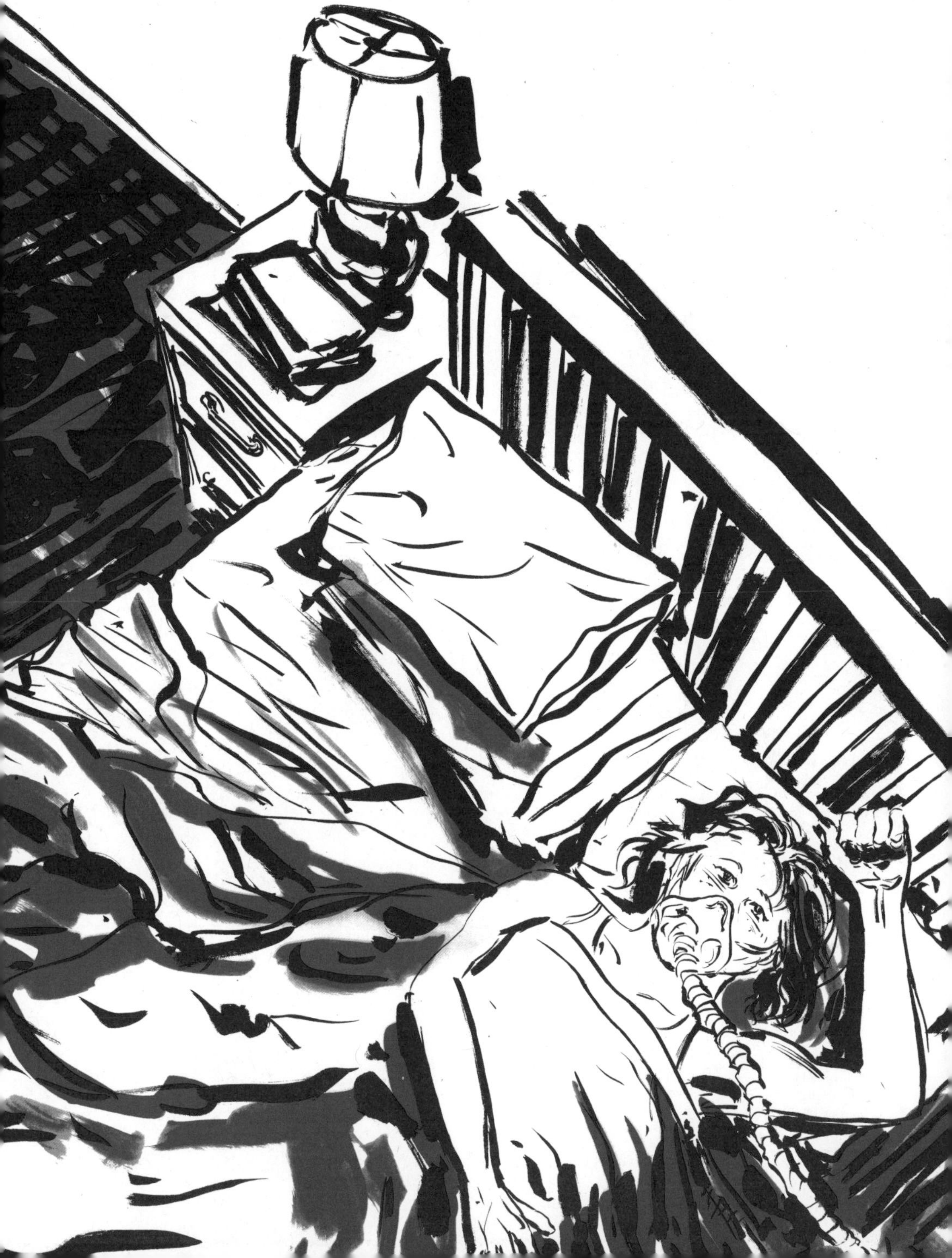

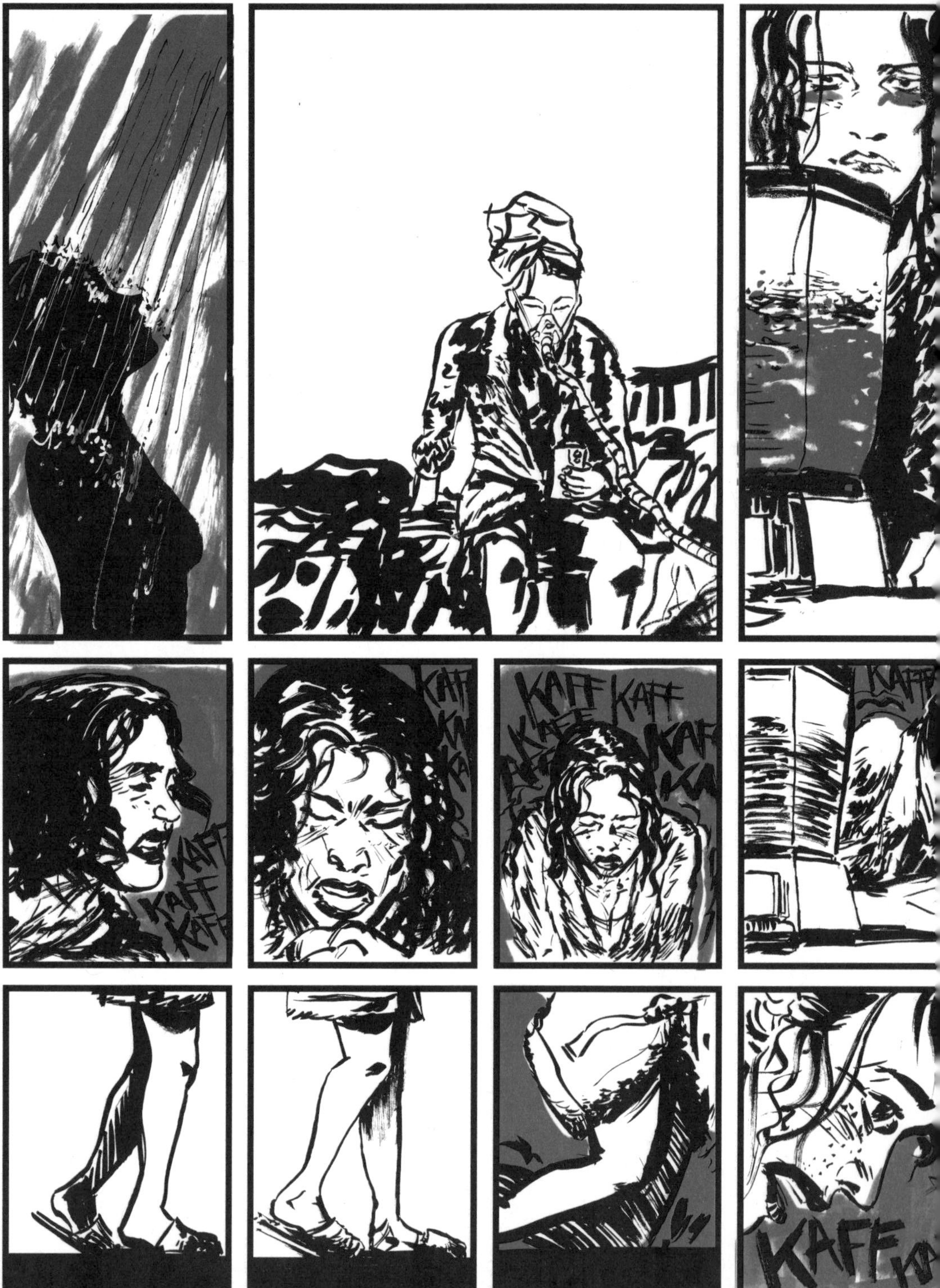
KAFF
KAFF
KAFF
KAFF
KAFF KAFF
KAFF
KAFF
KAFF

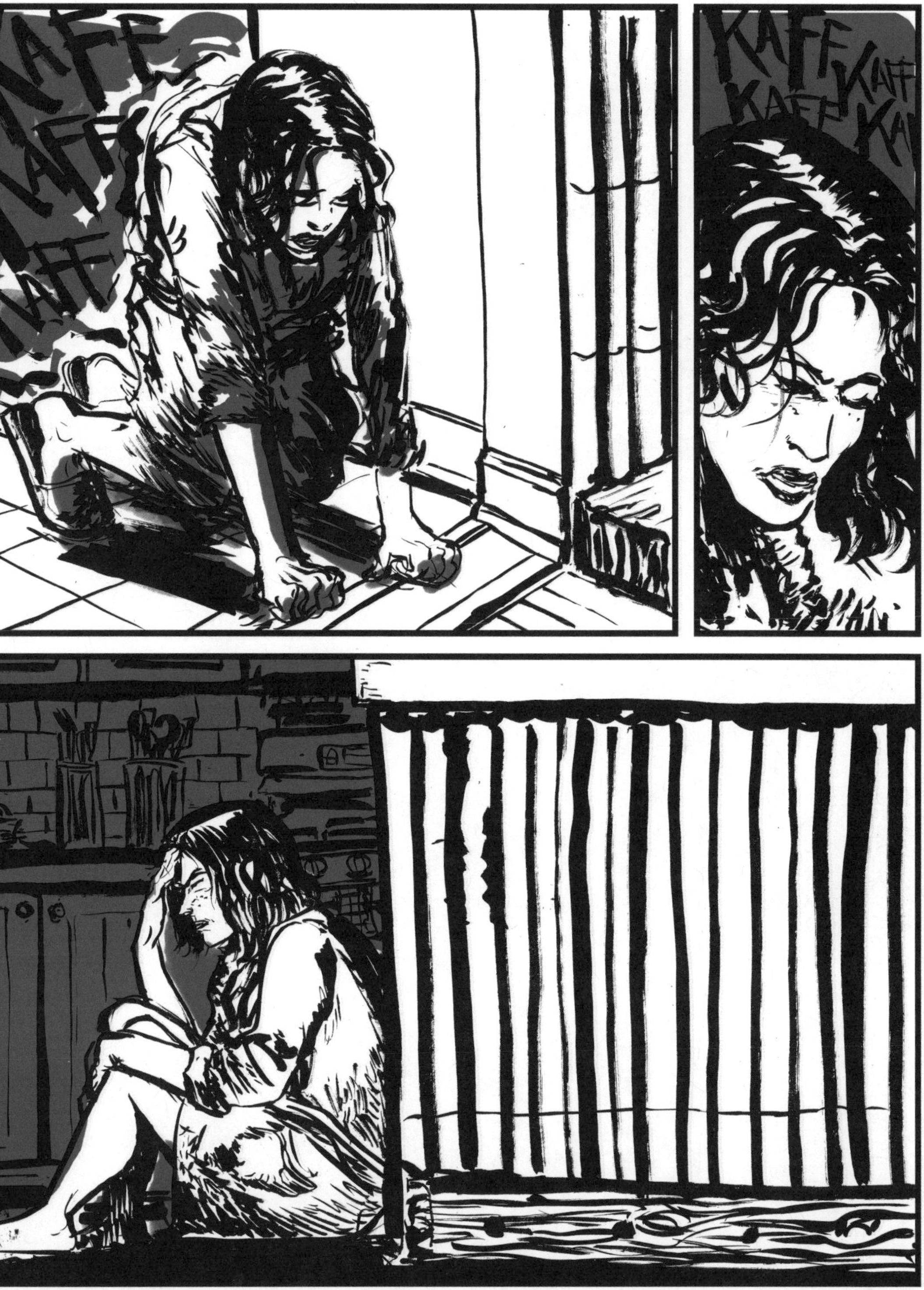

KAFF KAFF

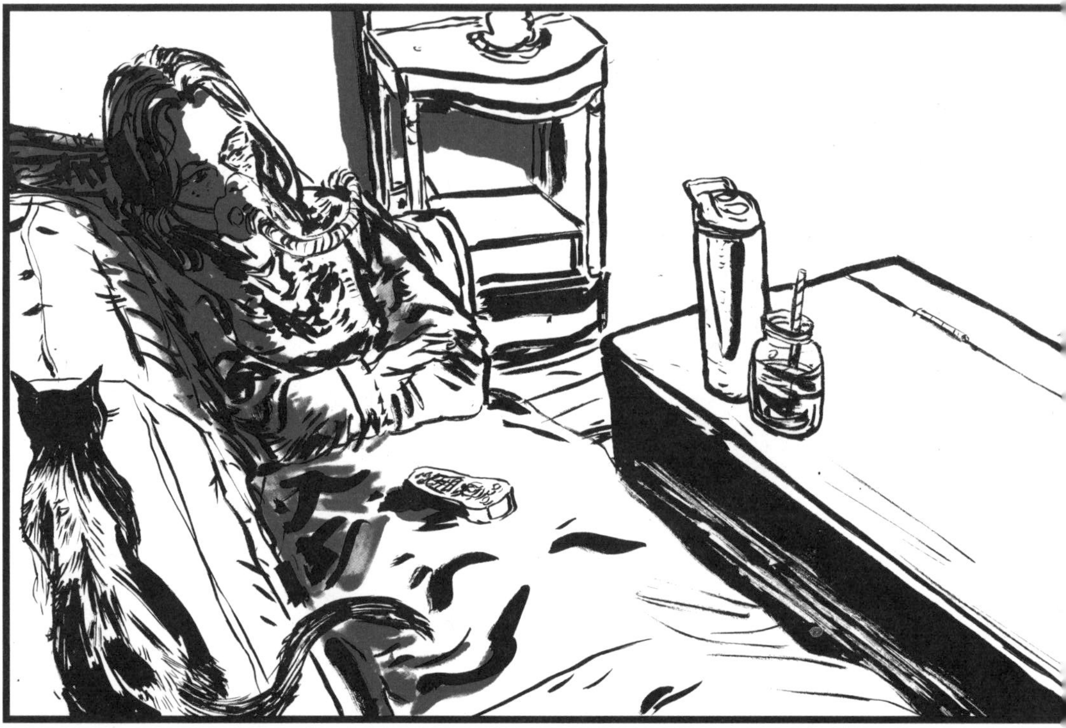
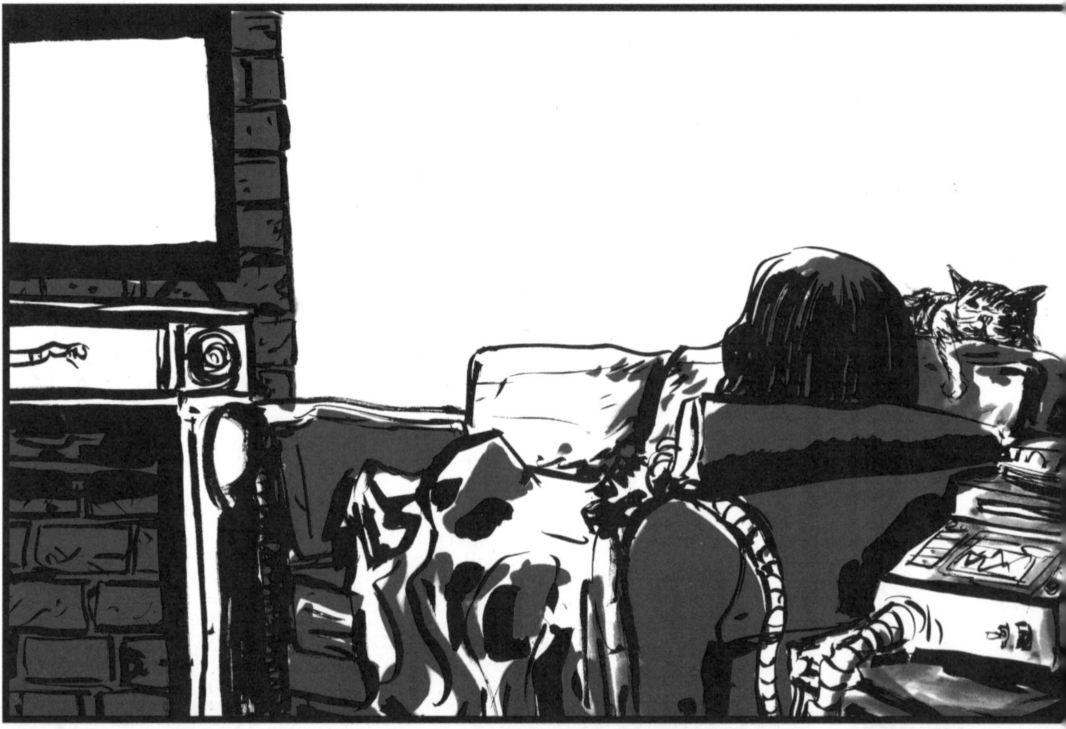

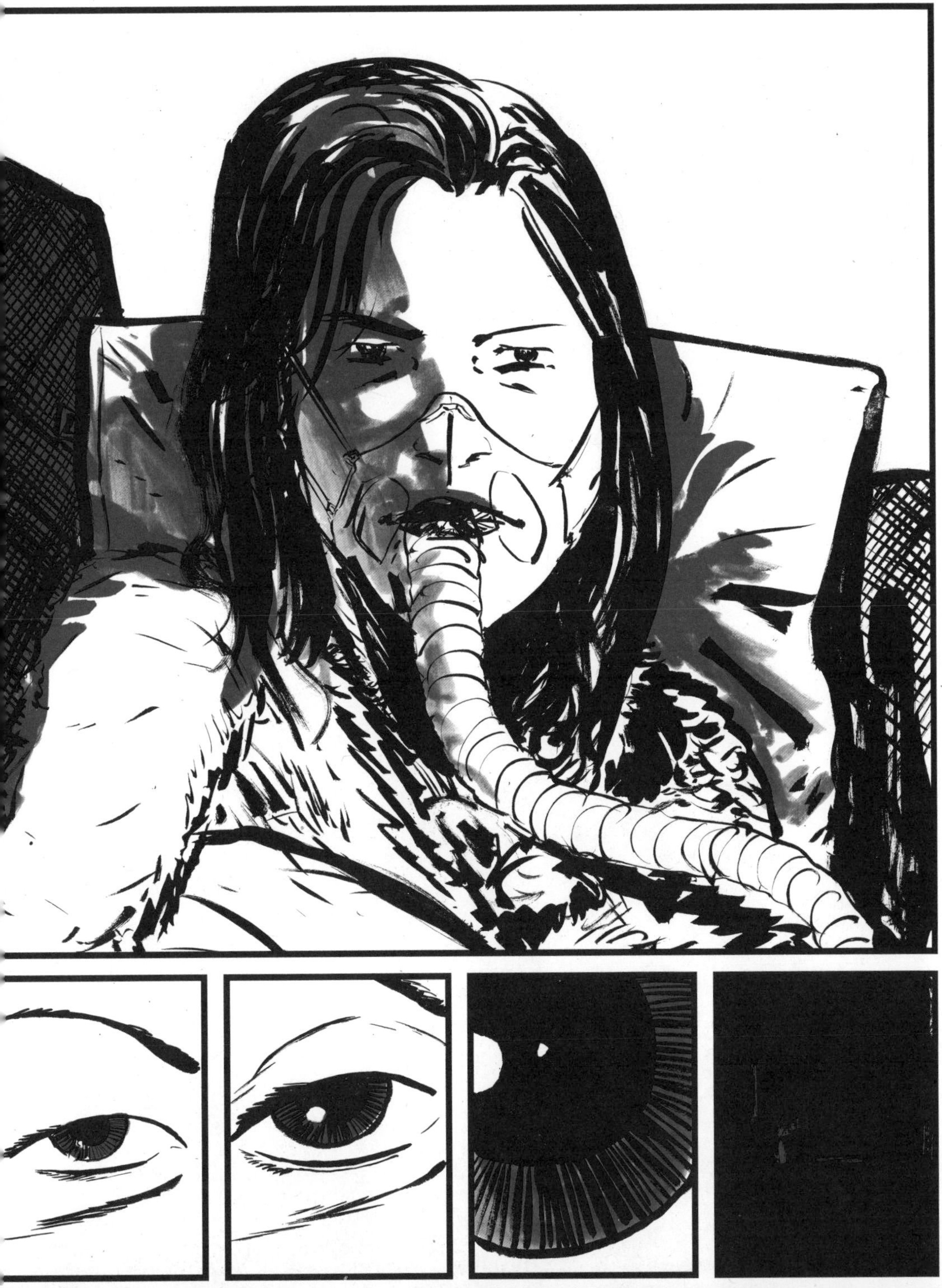

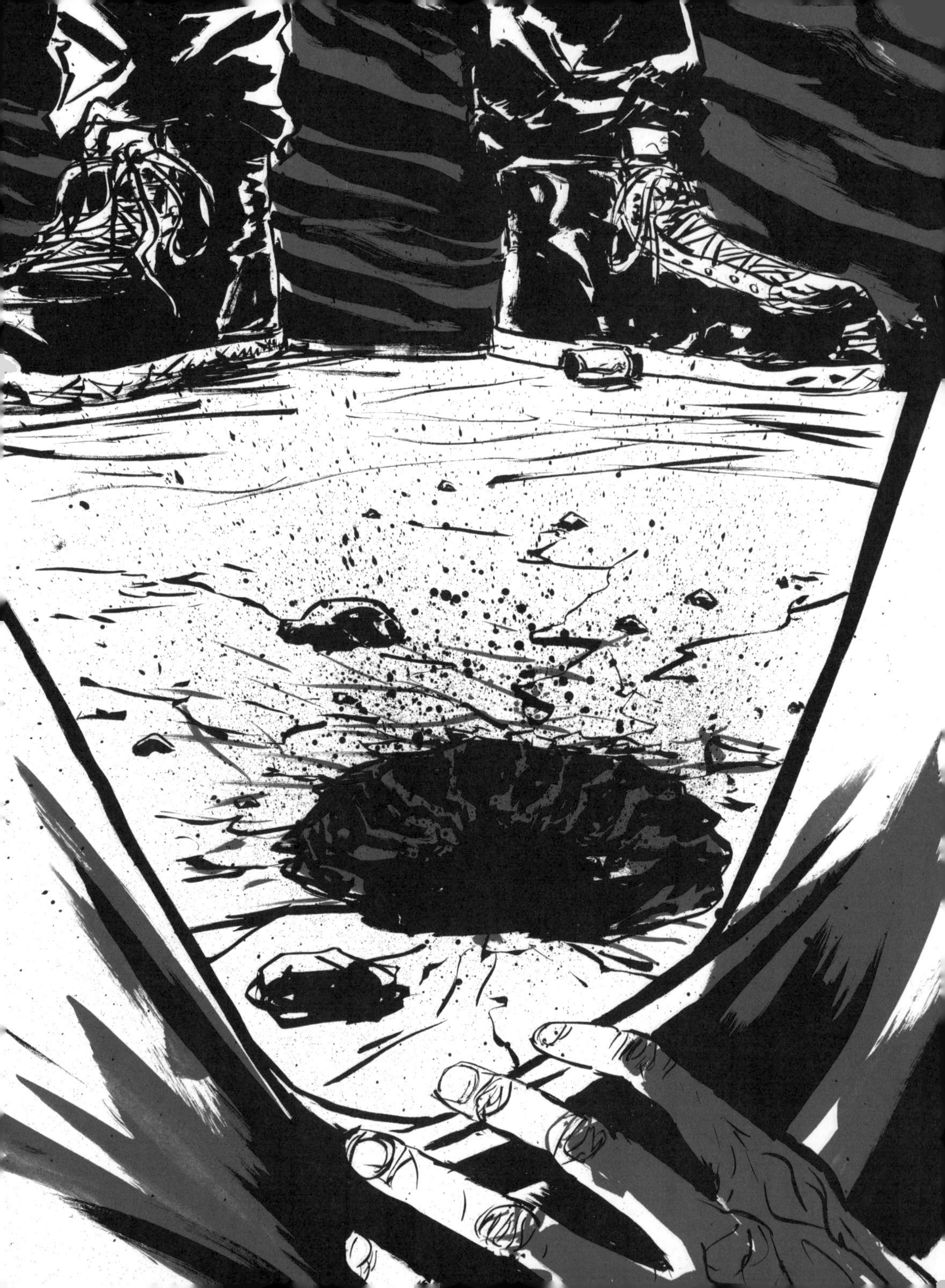

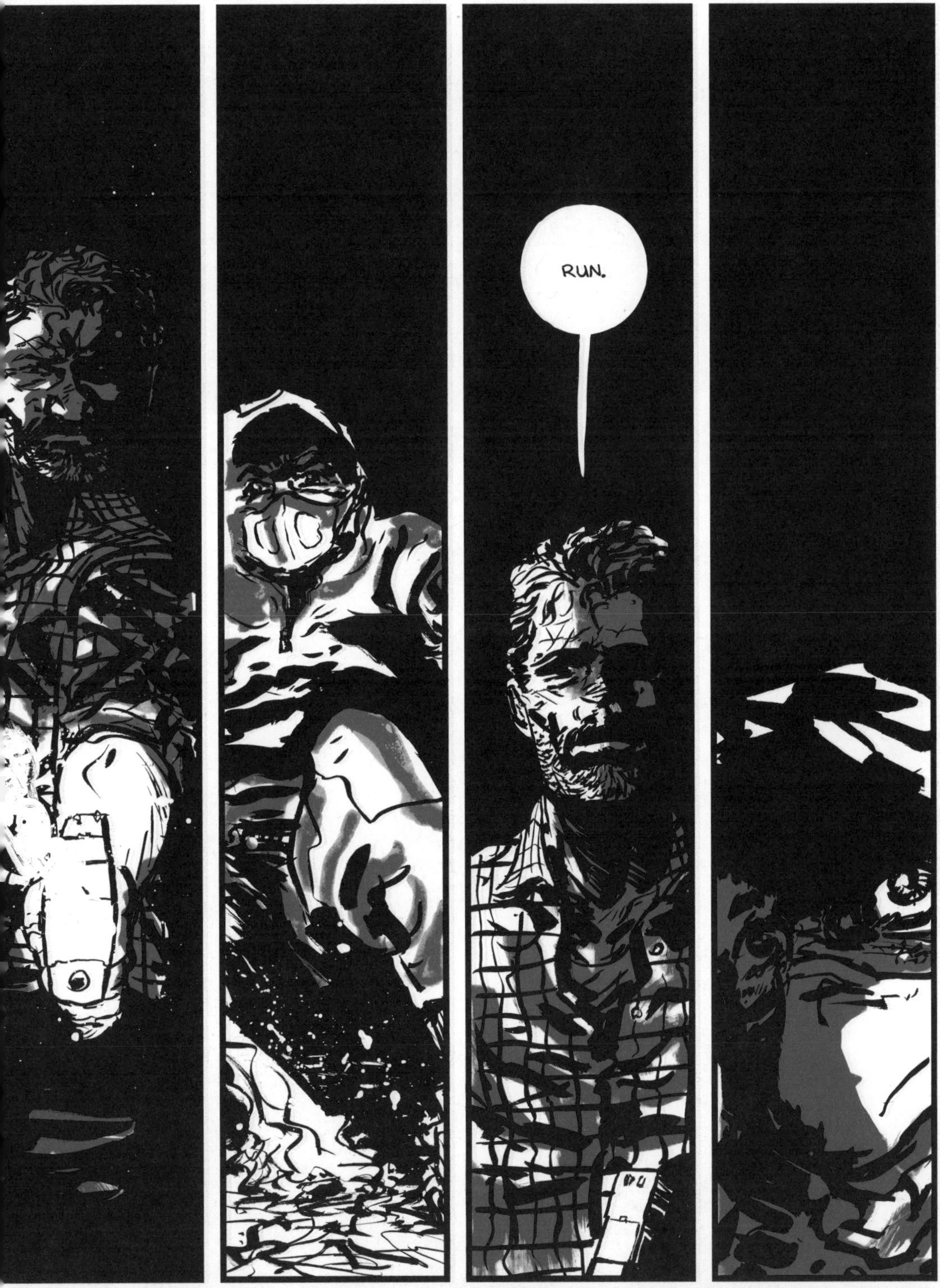
RUN.

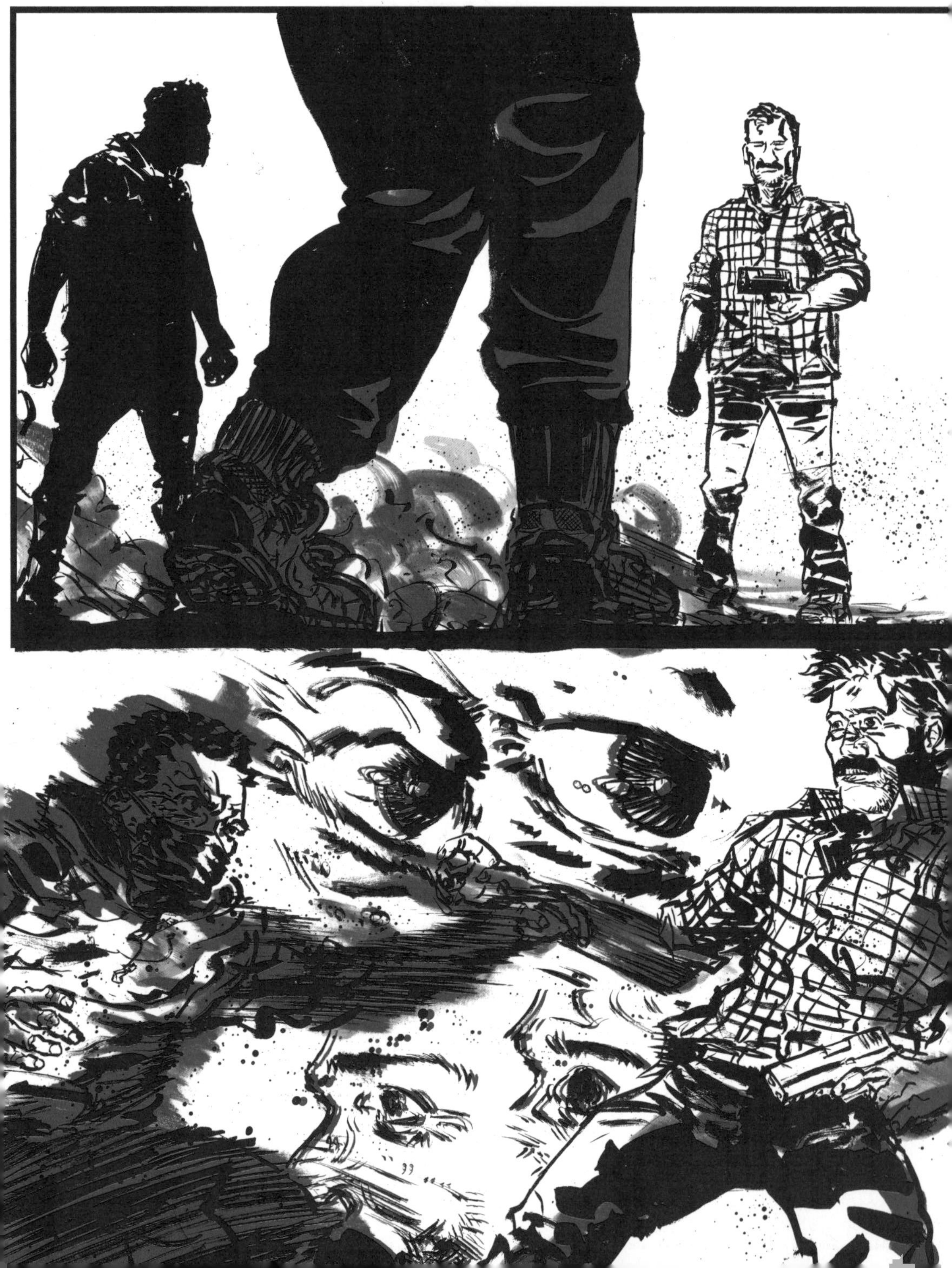

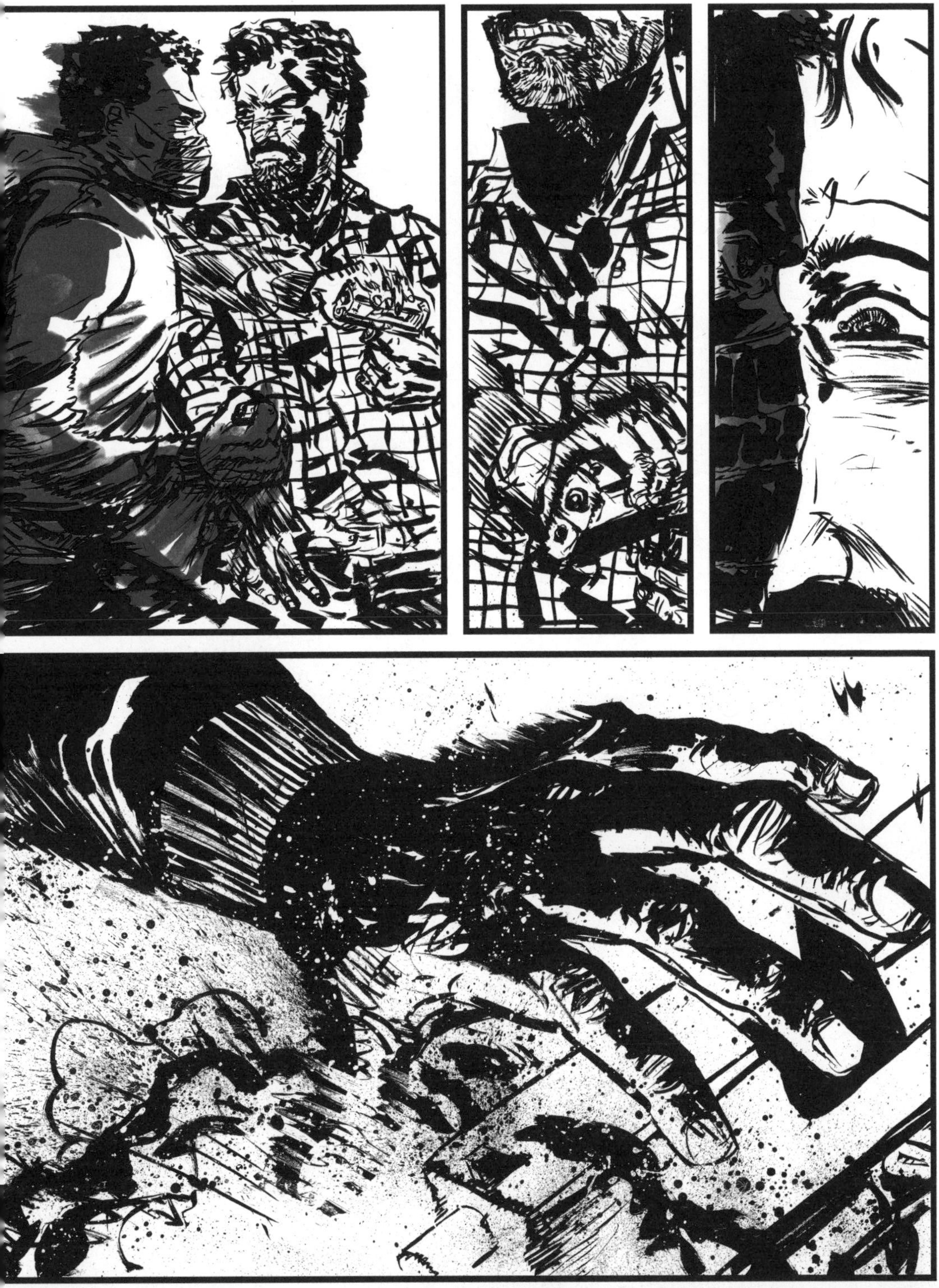

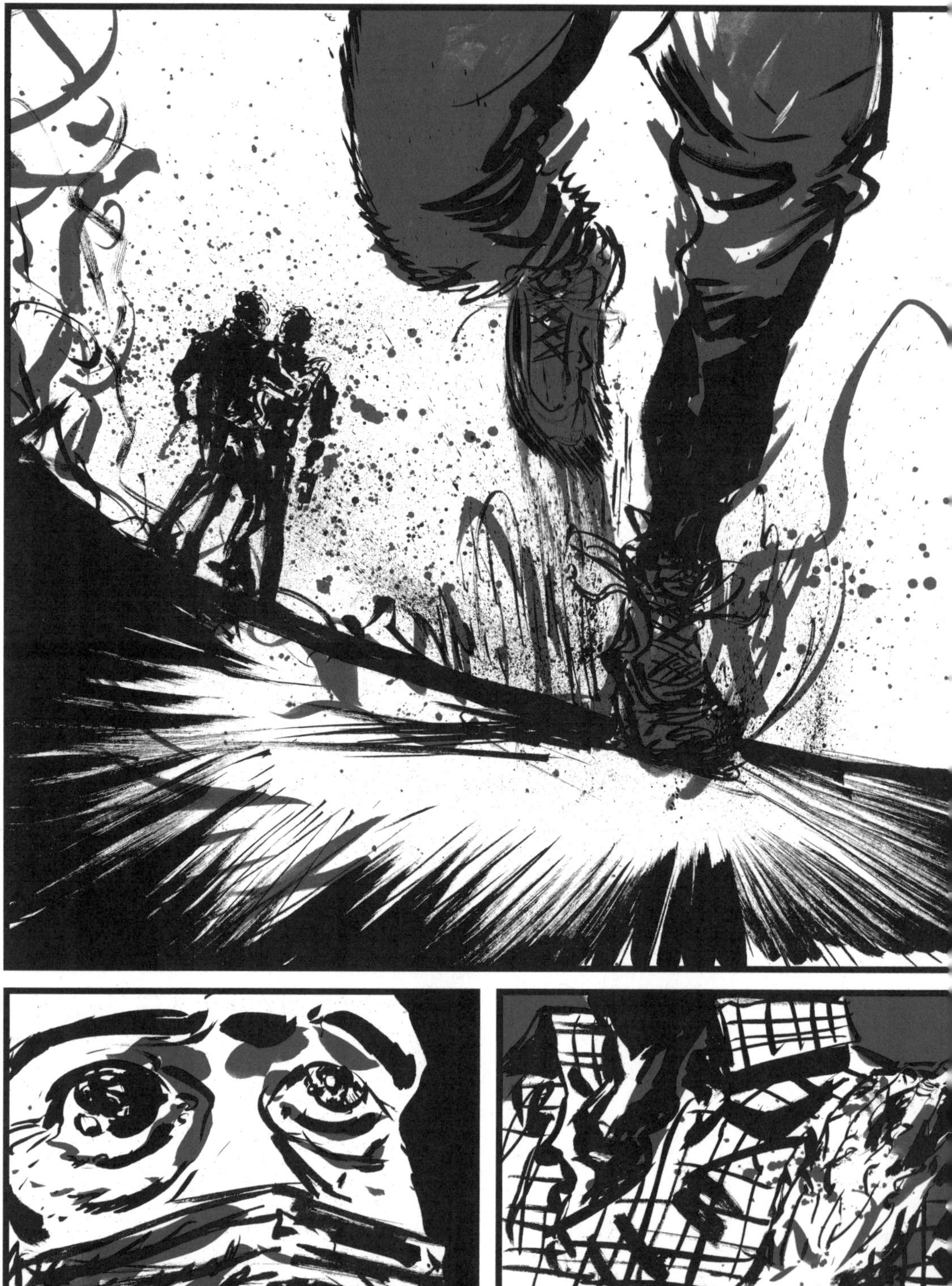

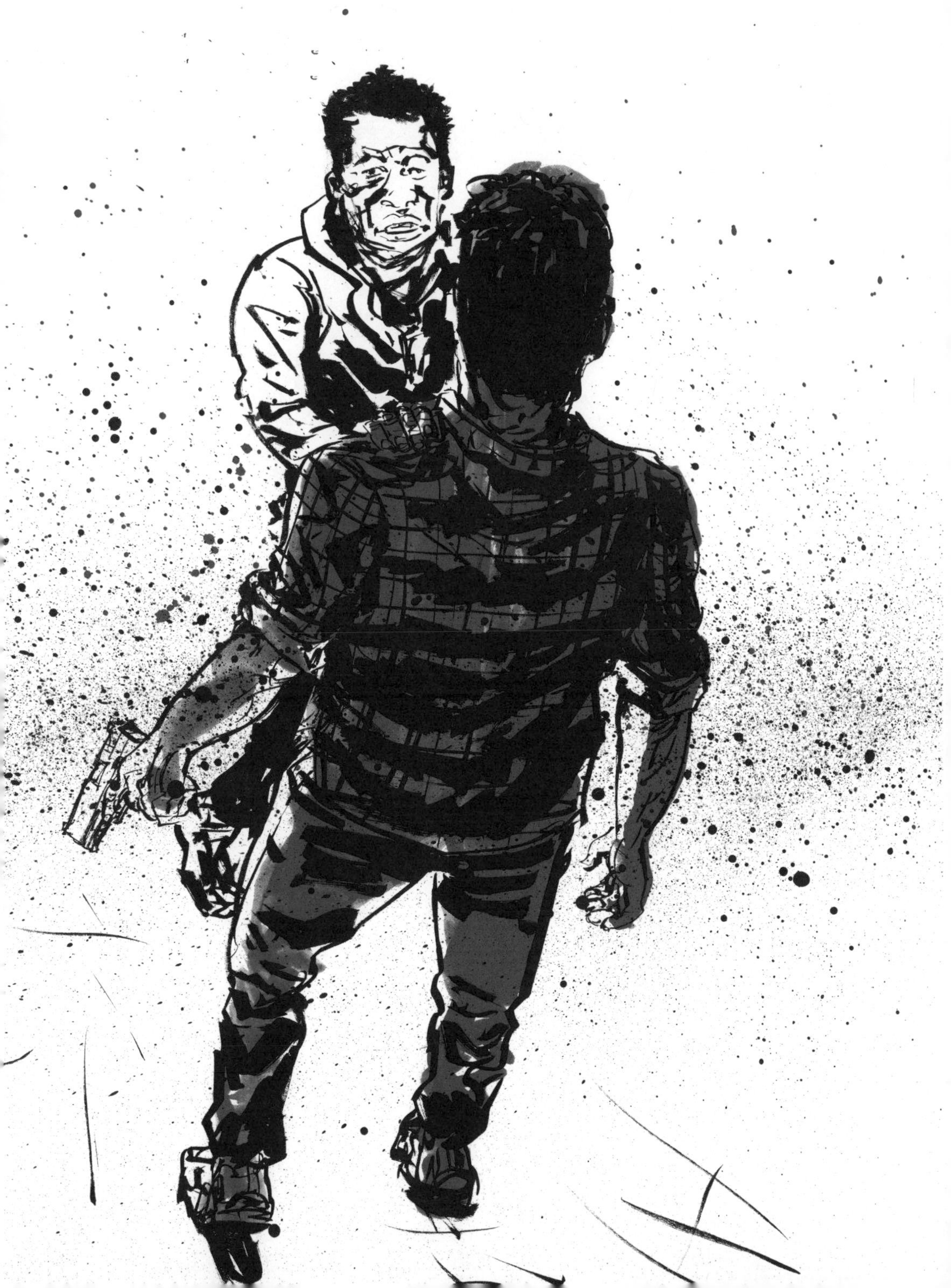

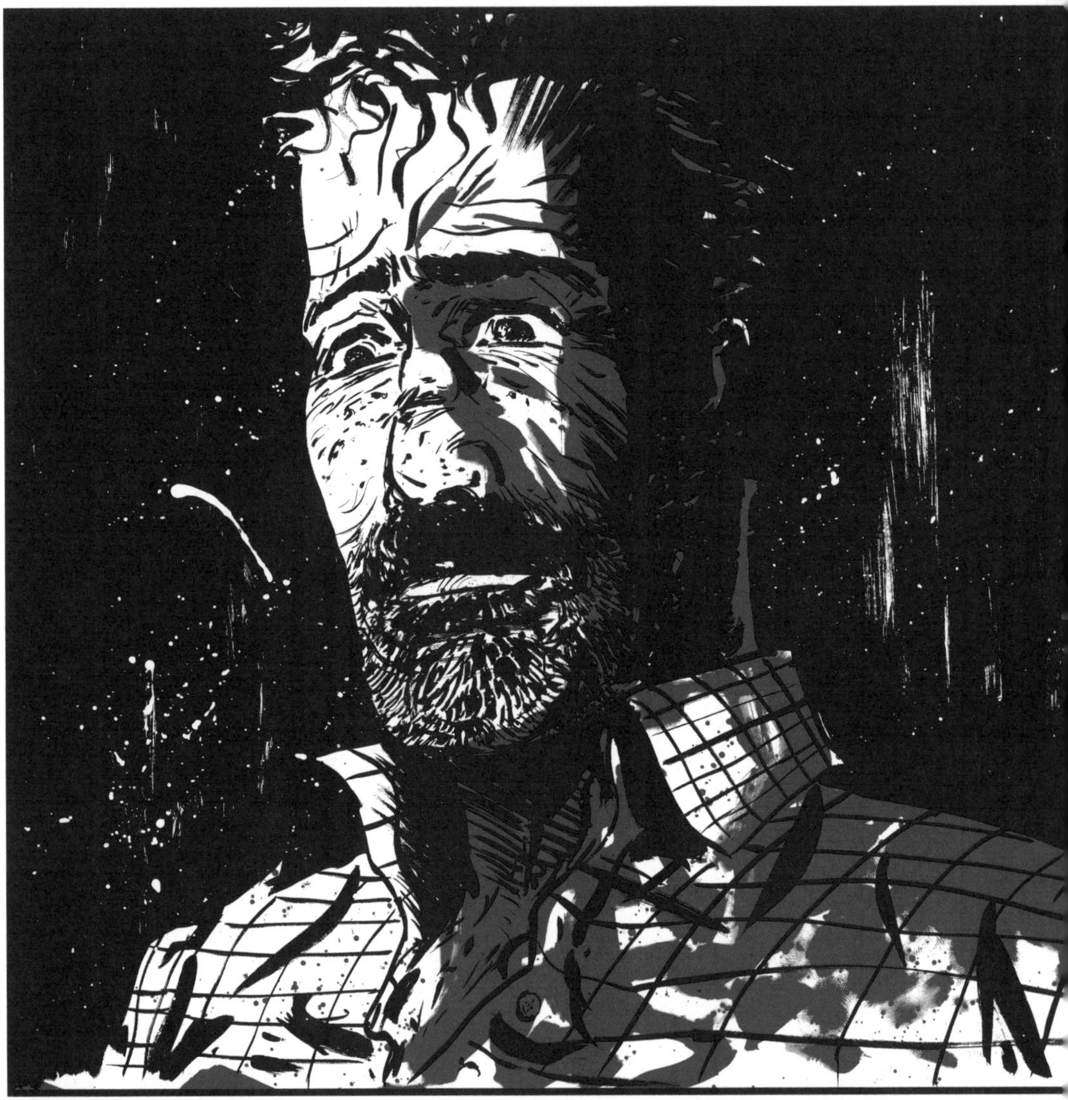
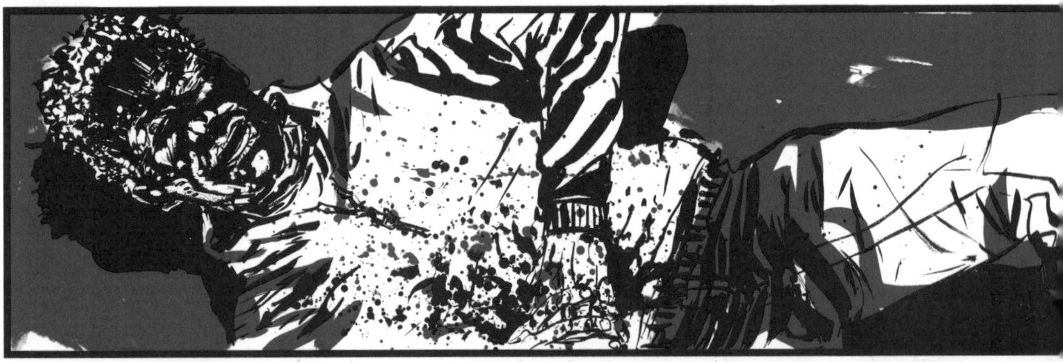

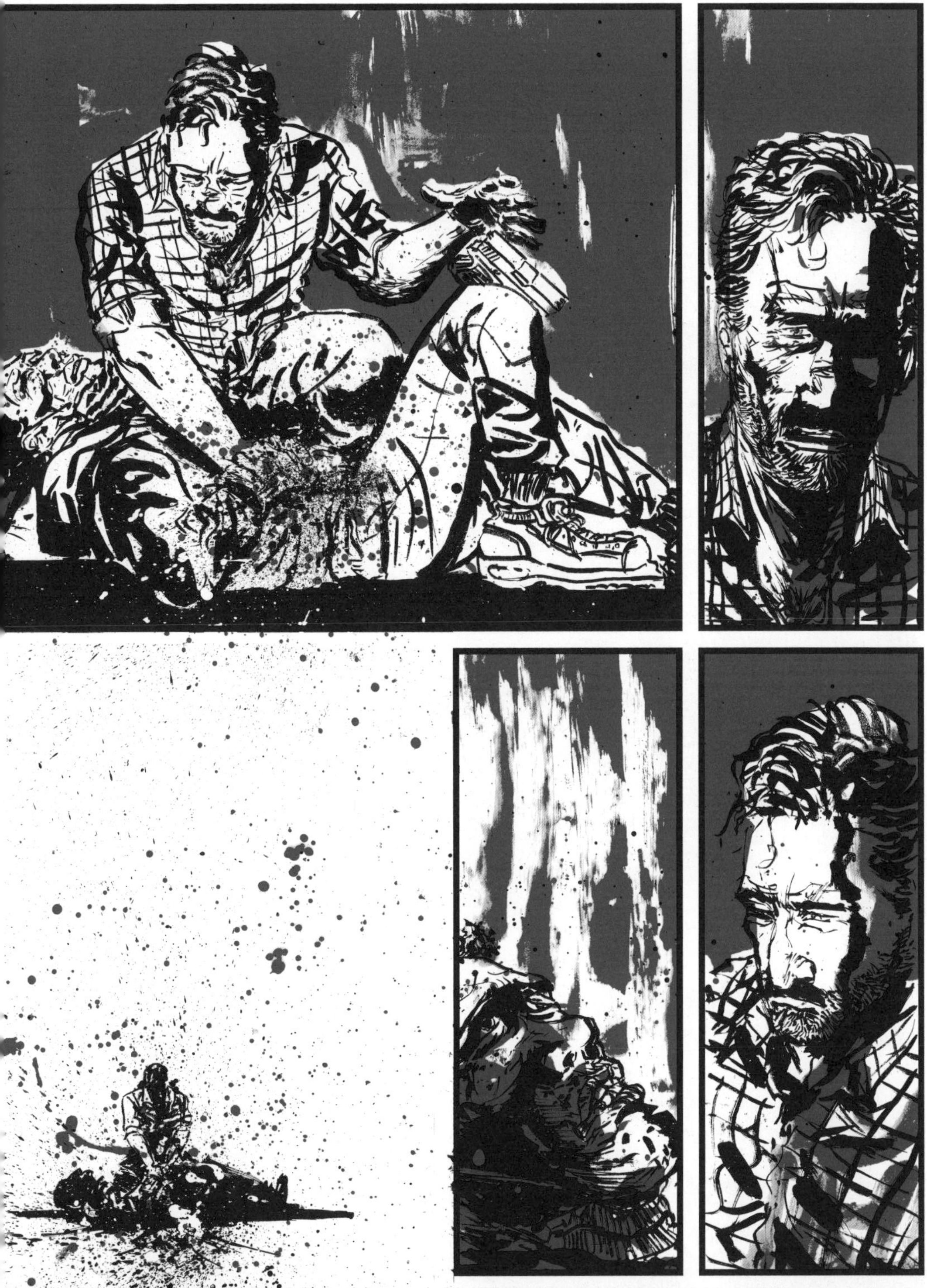

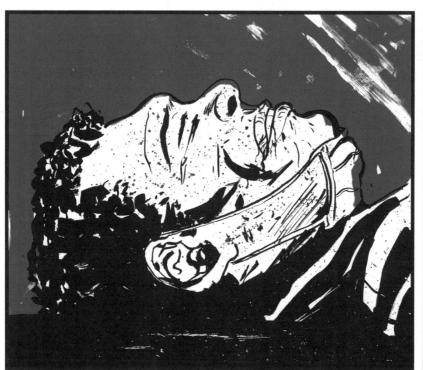

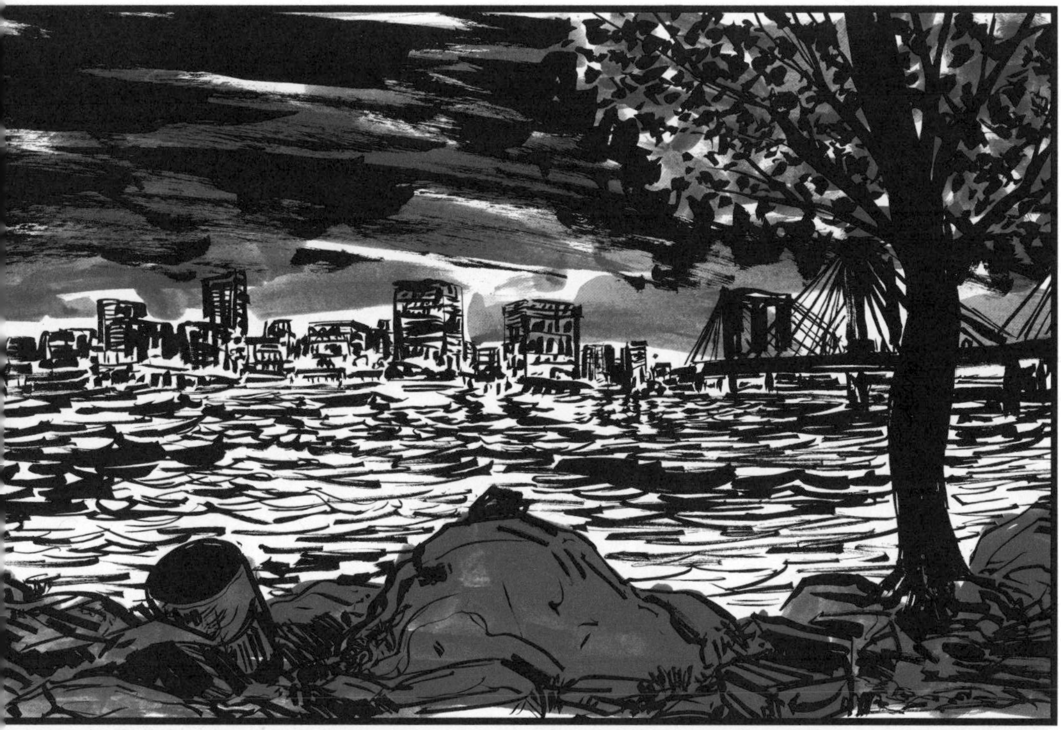

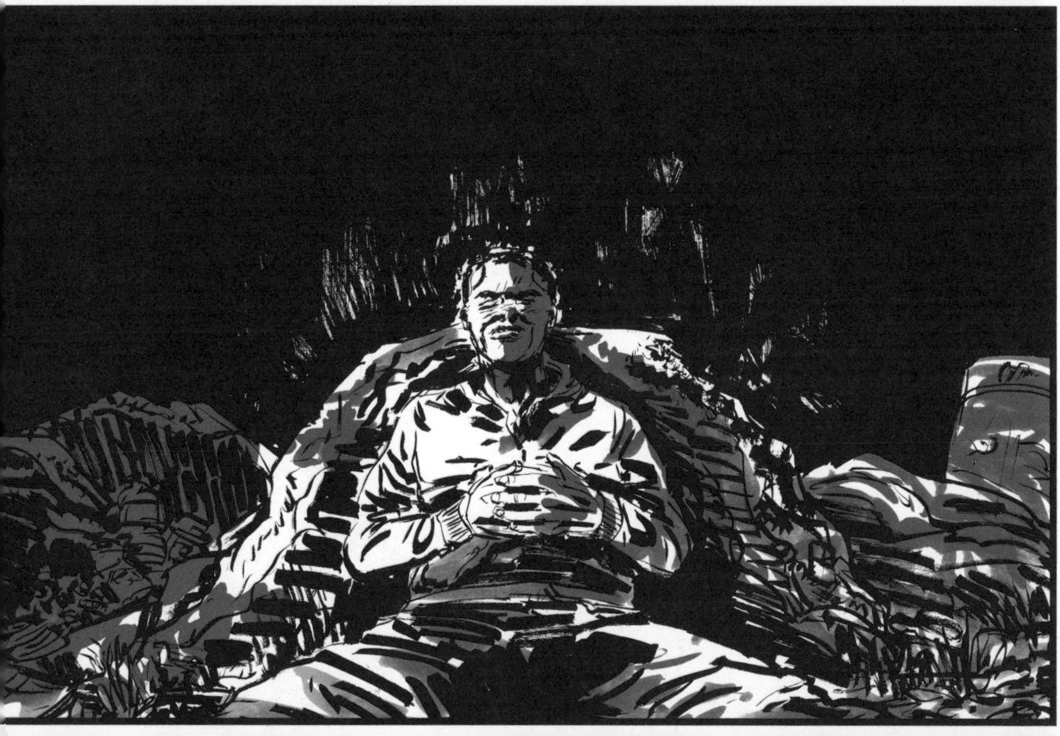

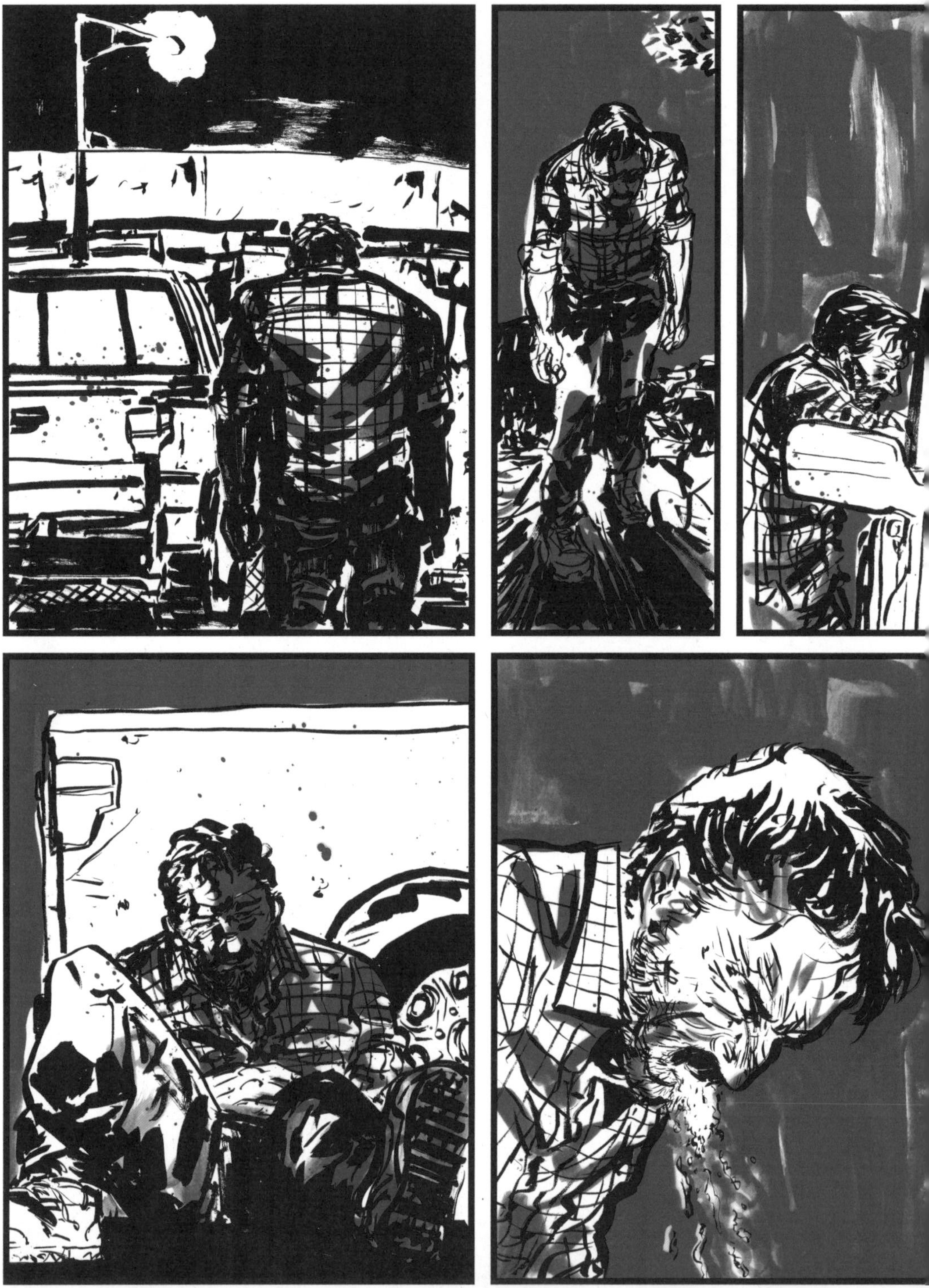

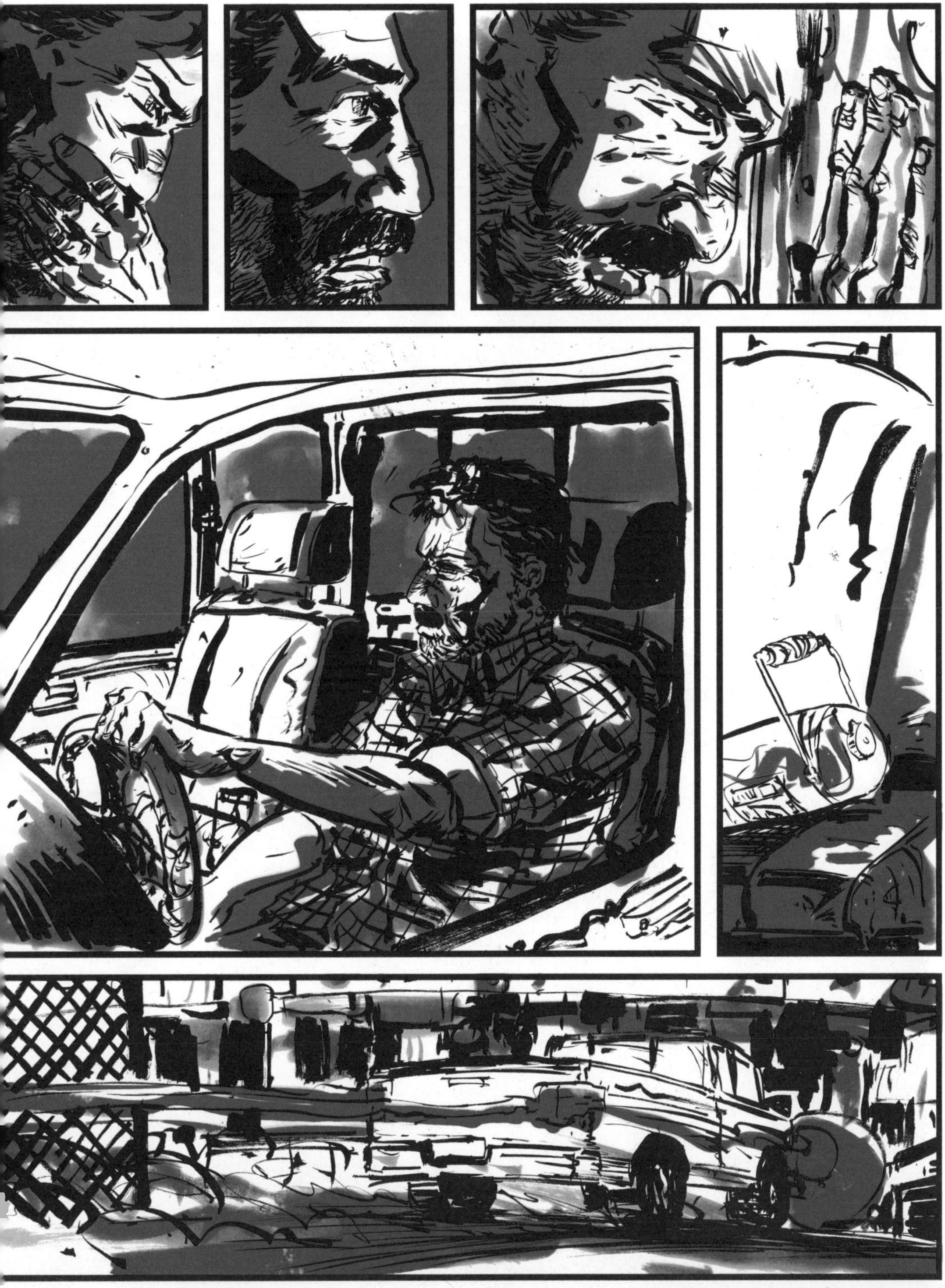

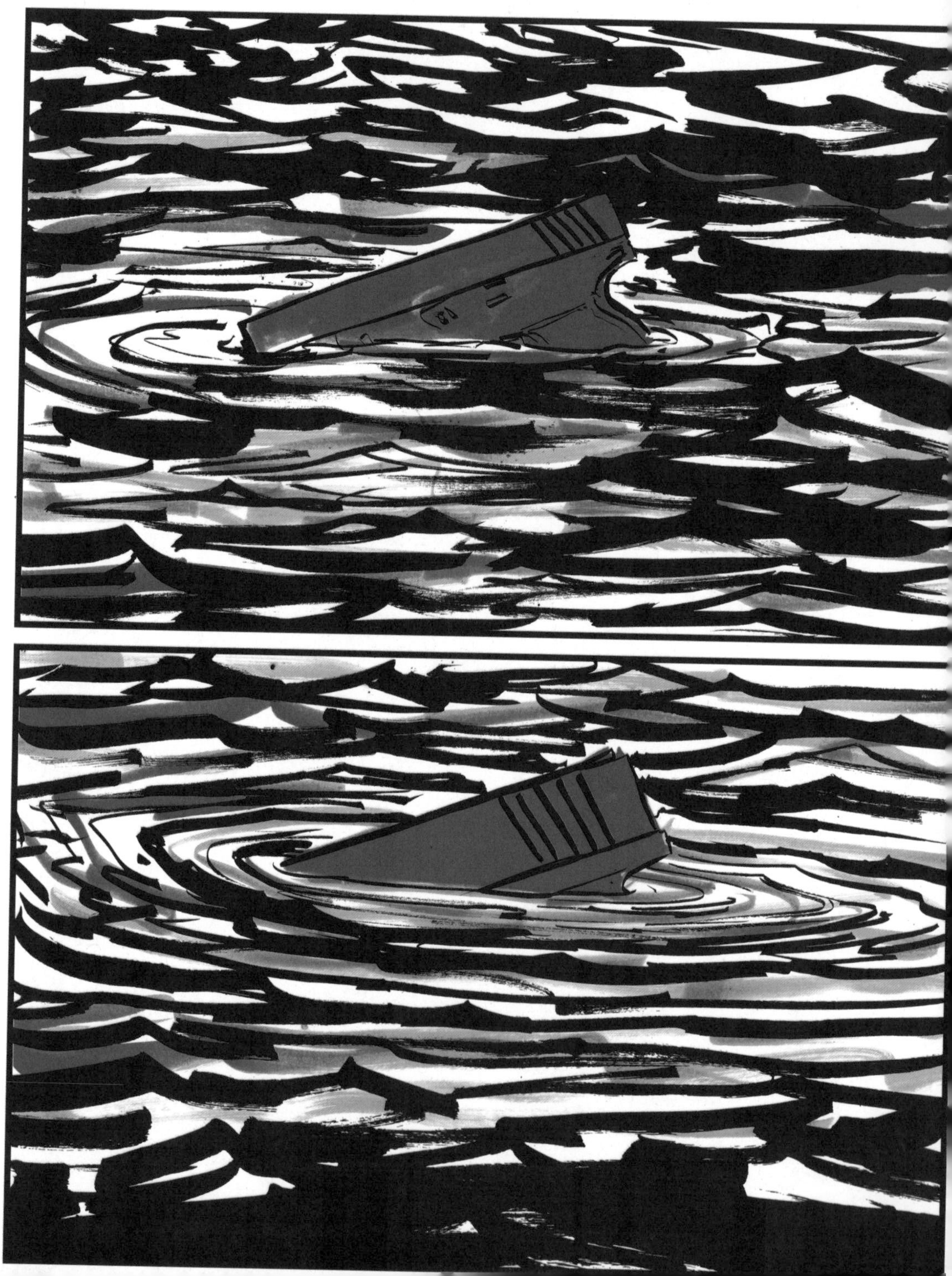

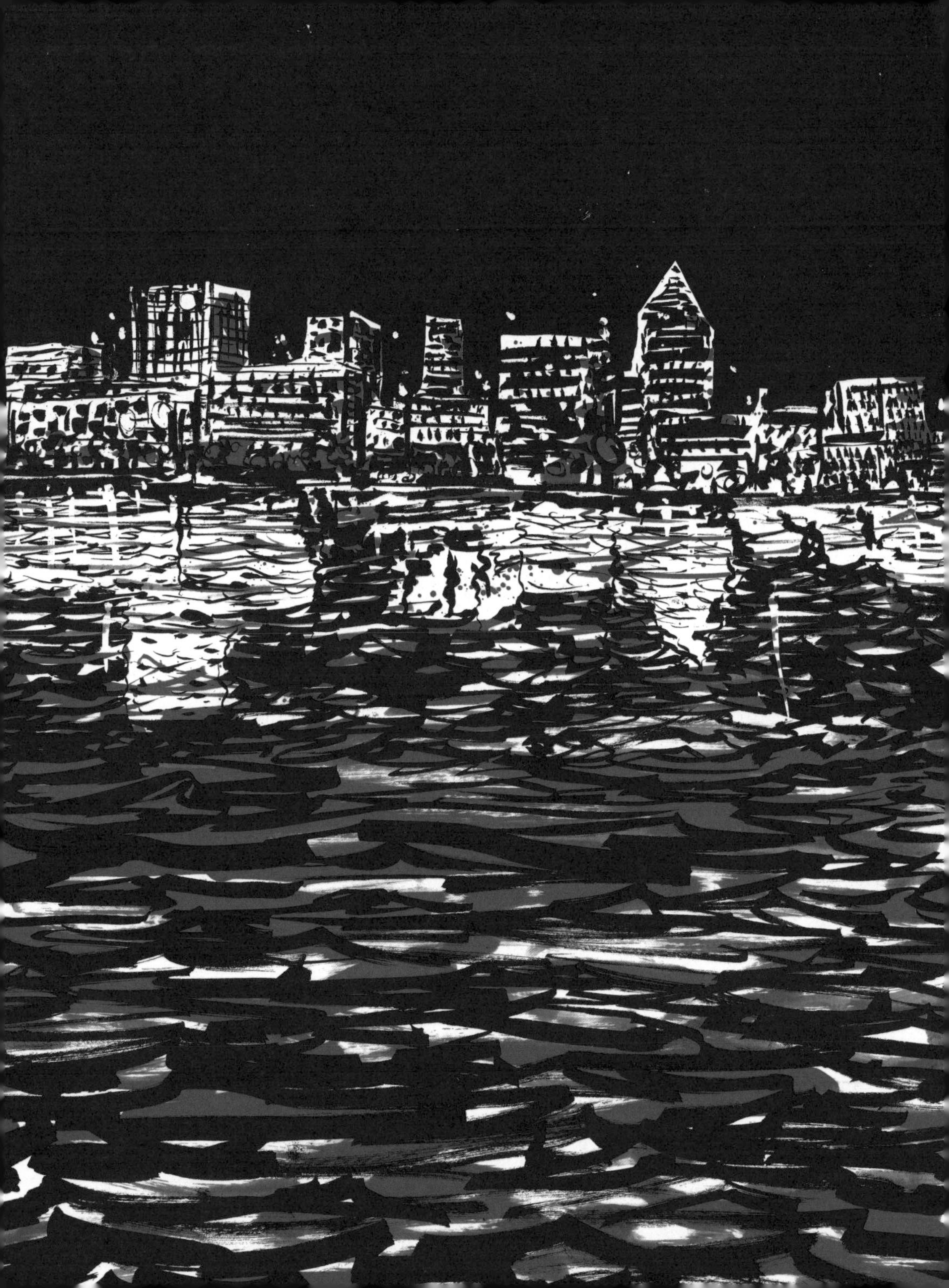

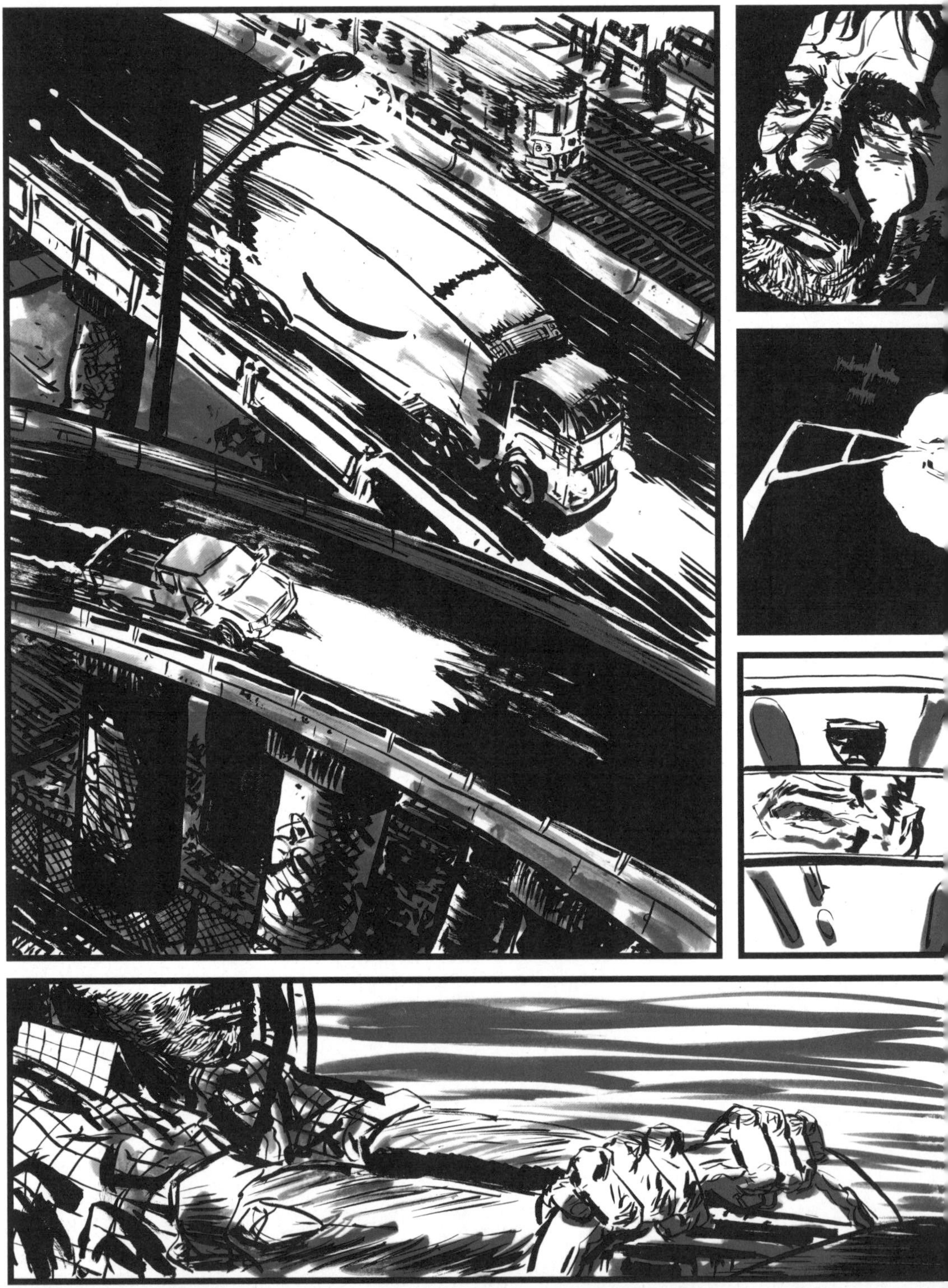

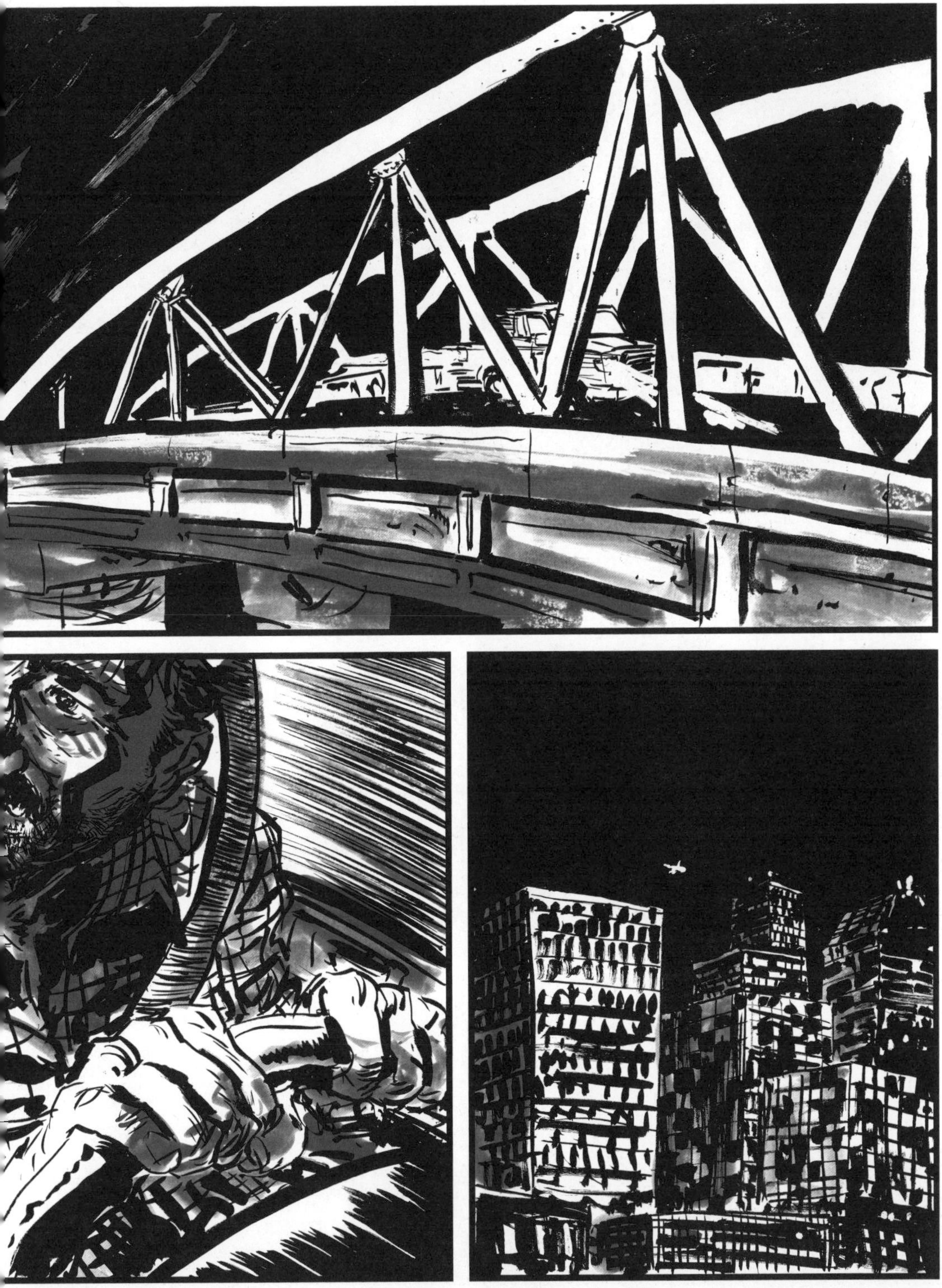

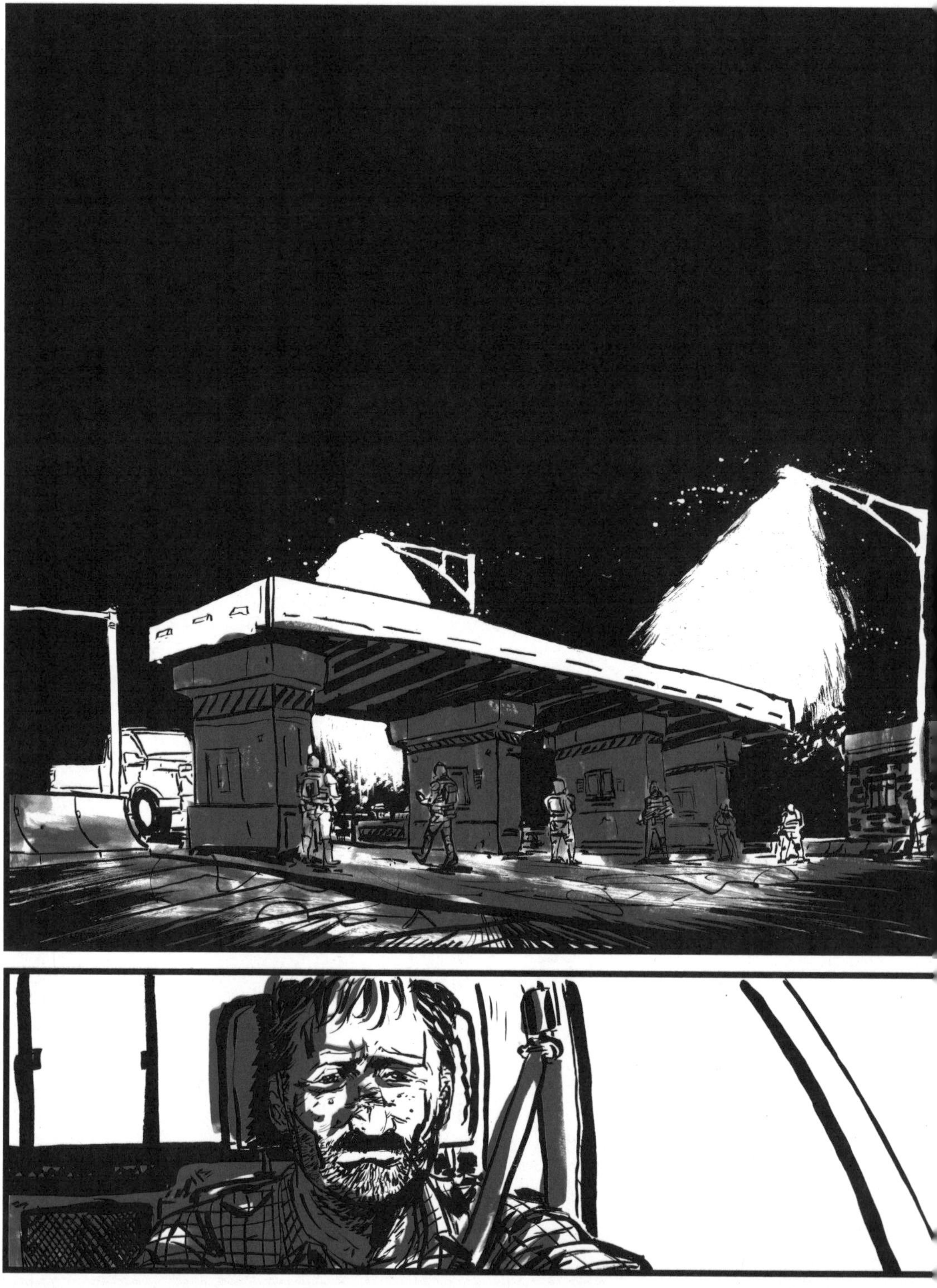

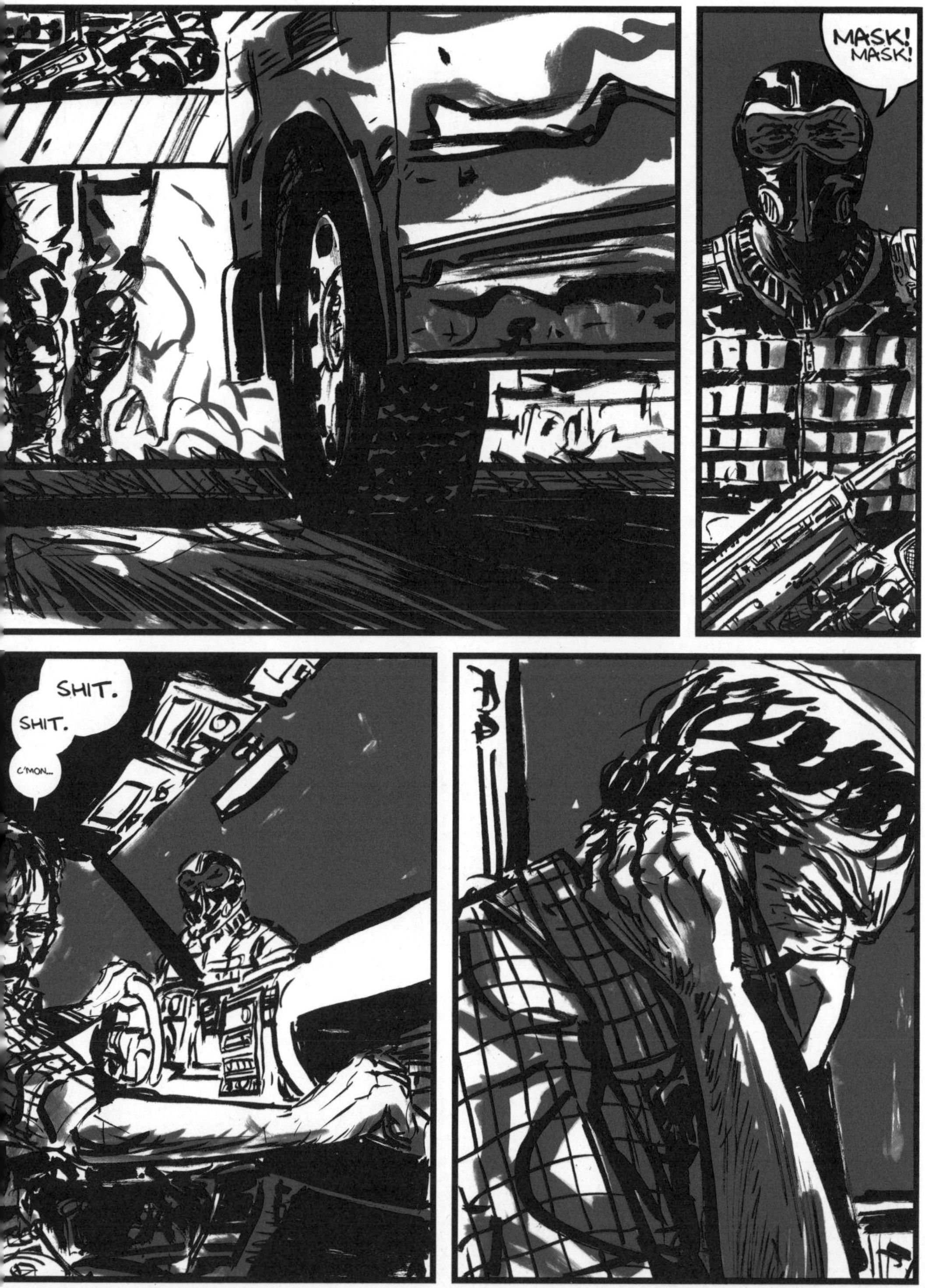
MASK! MASK!
SHIT.
SHIT.
C'MON...

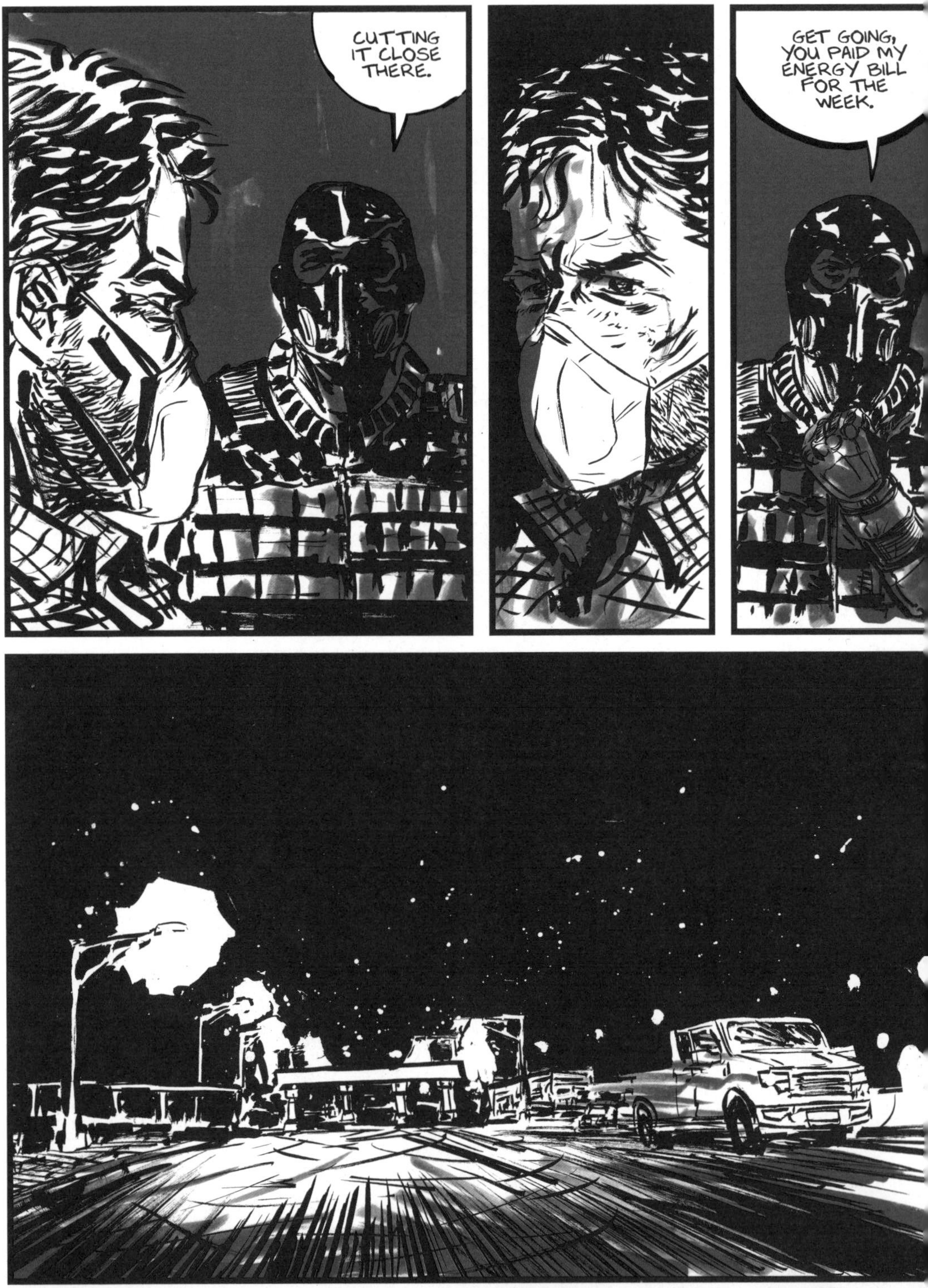
CUTTING IT CLOSE THERE.
GET GOING, YOU PAID MY ENERGY BILL FOR THE WEEK.

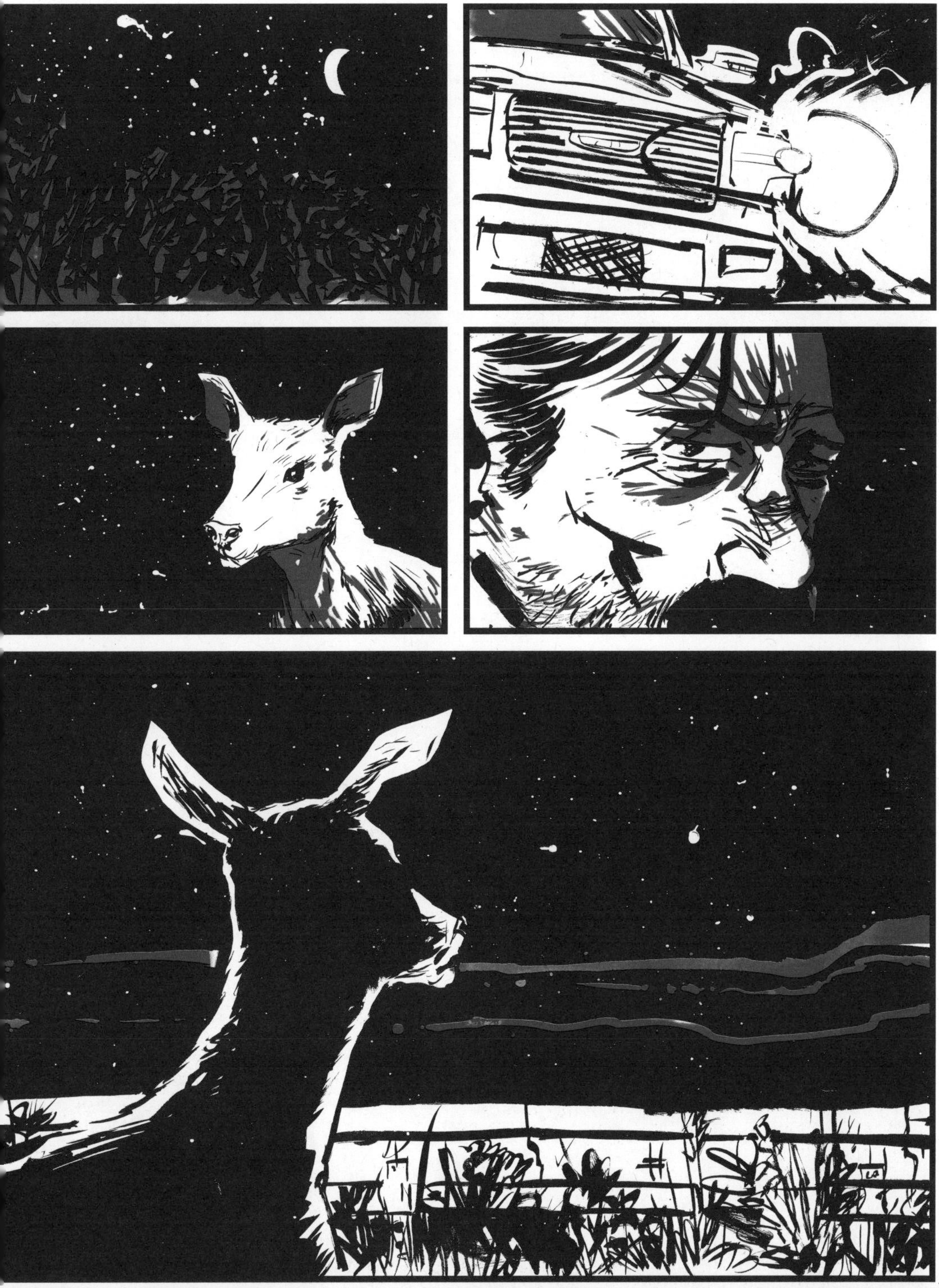

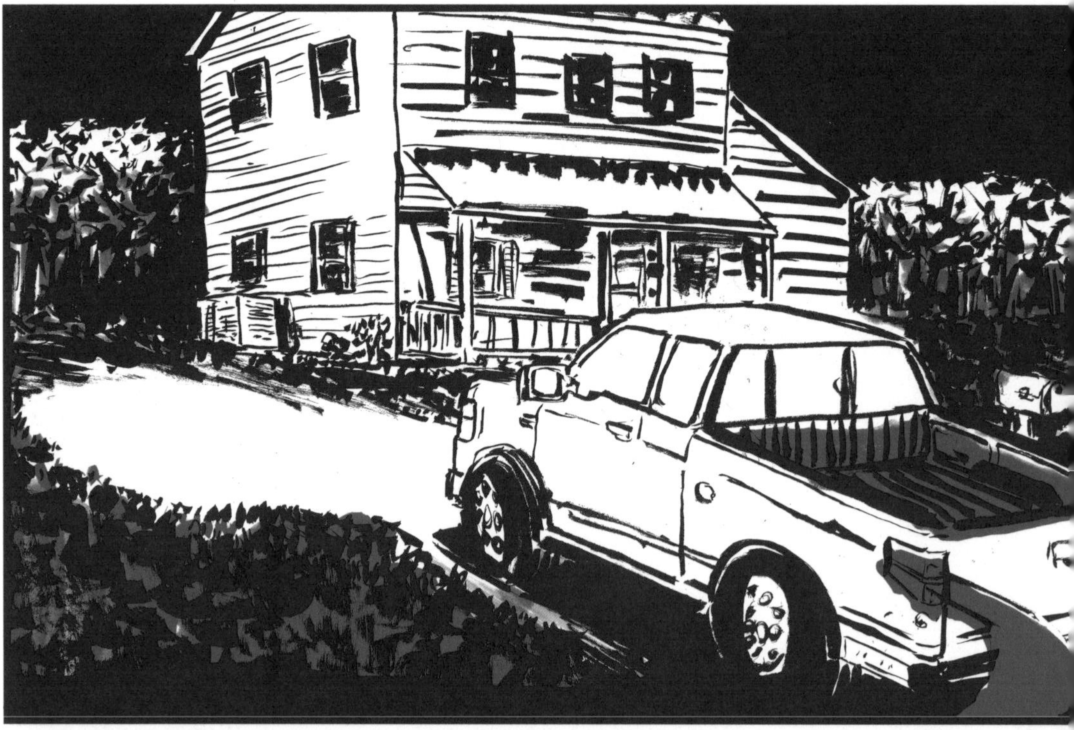

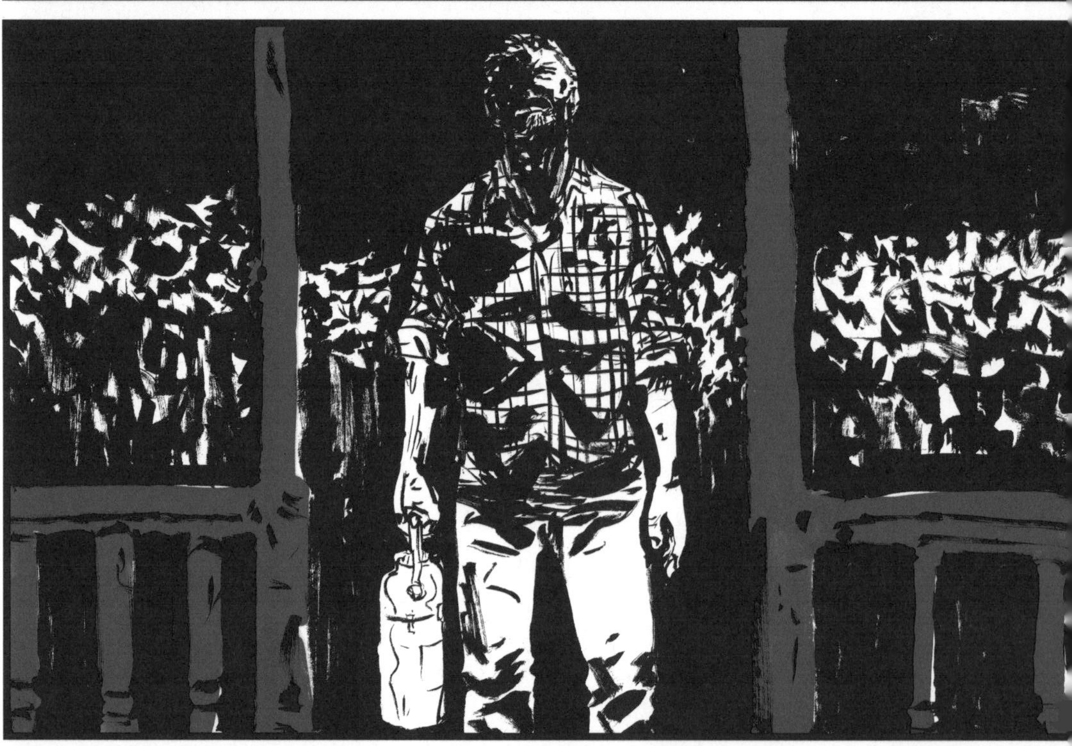

...I TRIED TO STAY UP...

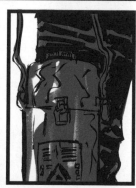

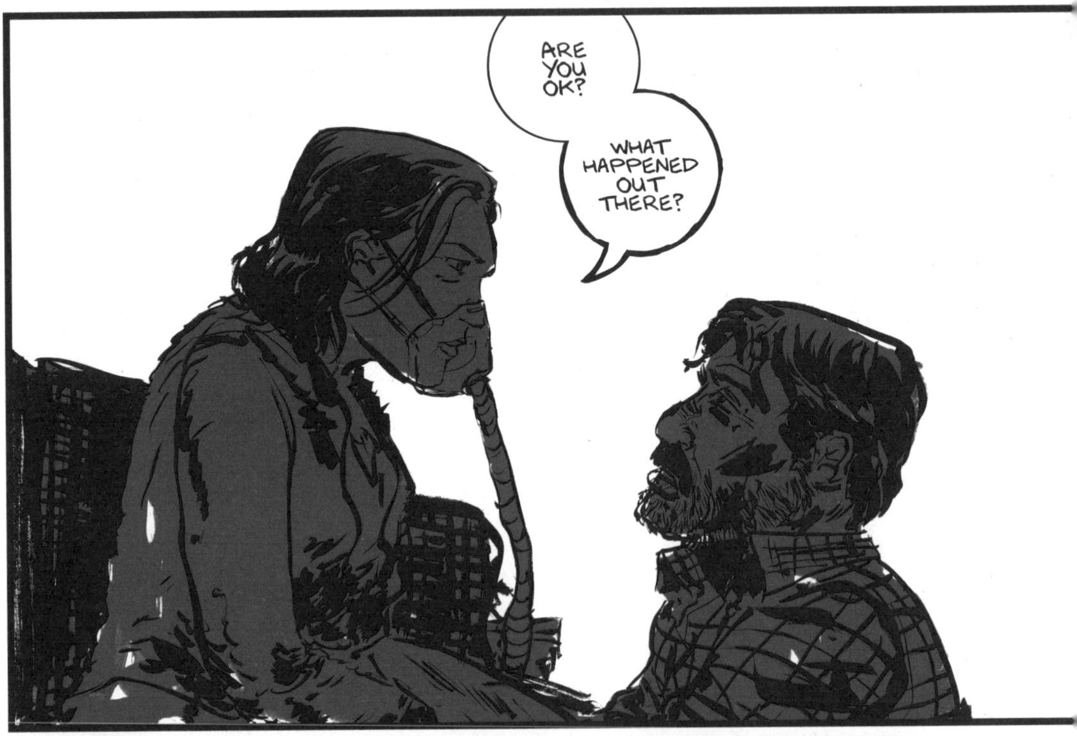
ARE YOU OK?
WHAT HAPPENED OUT THERE?

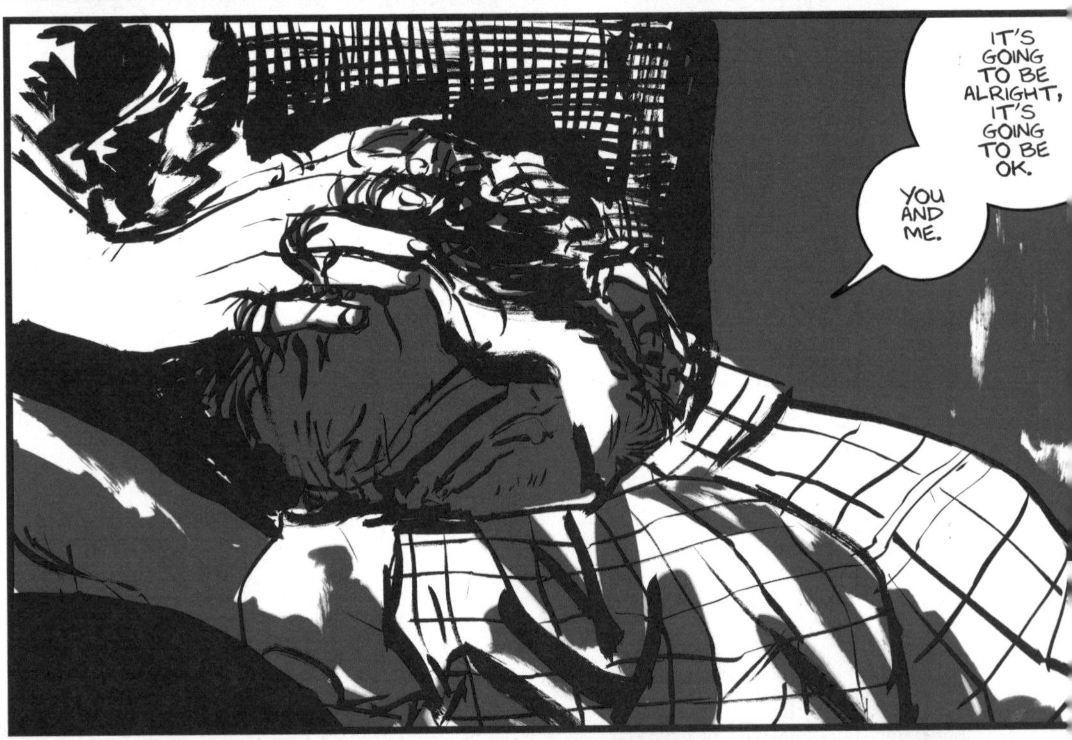
IT'S GOING TO BE ALRIGHT, IT'S GOING TO BE OK.
YOU AND ME.

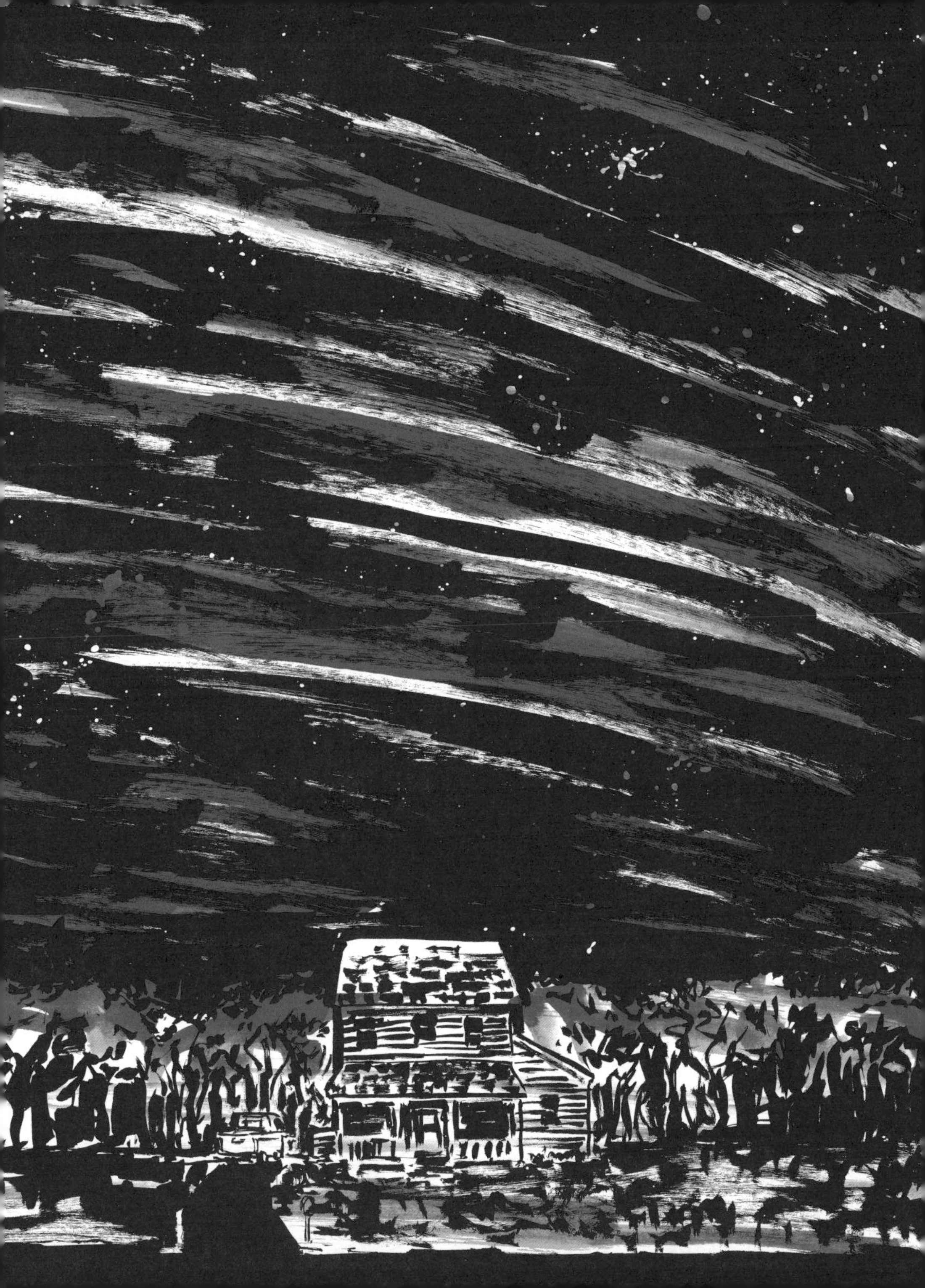

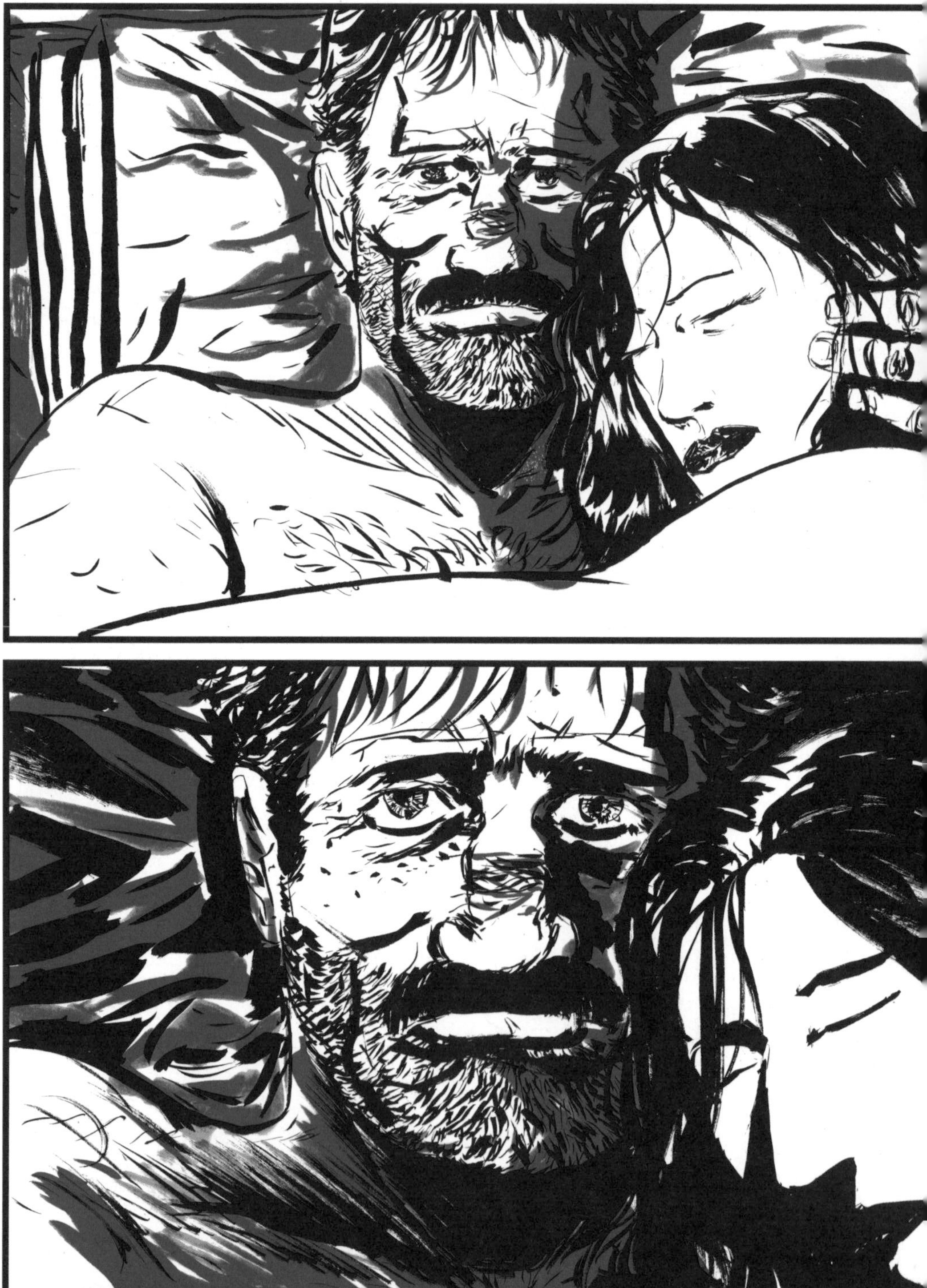

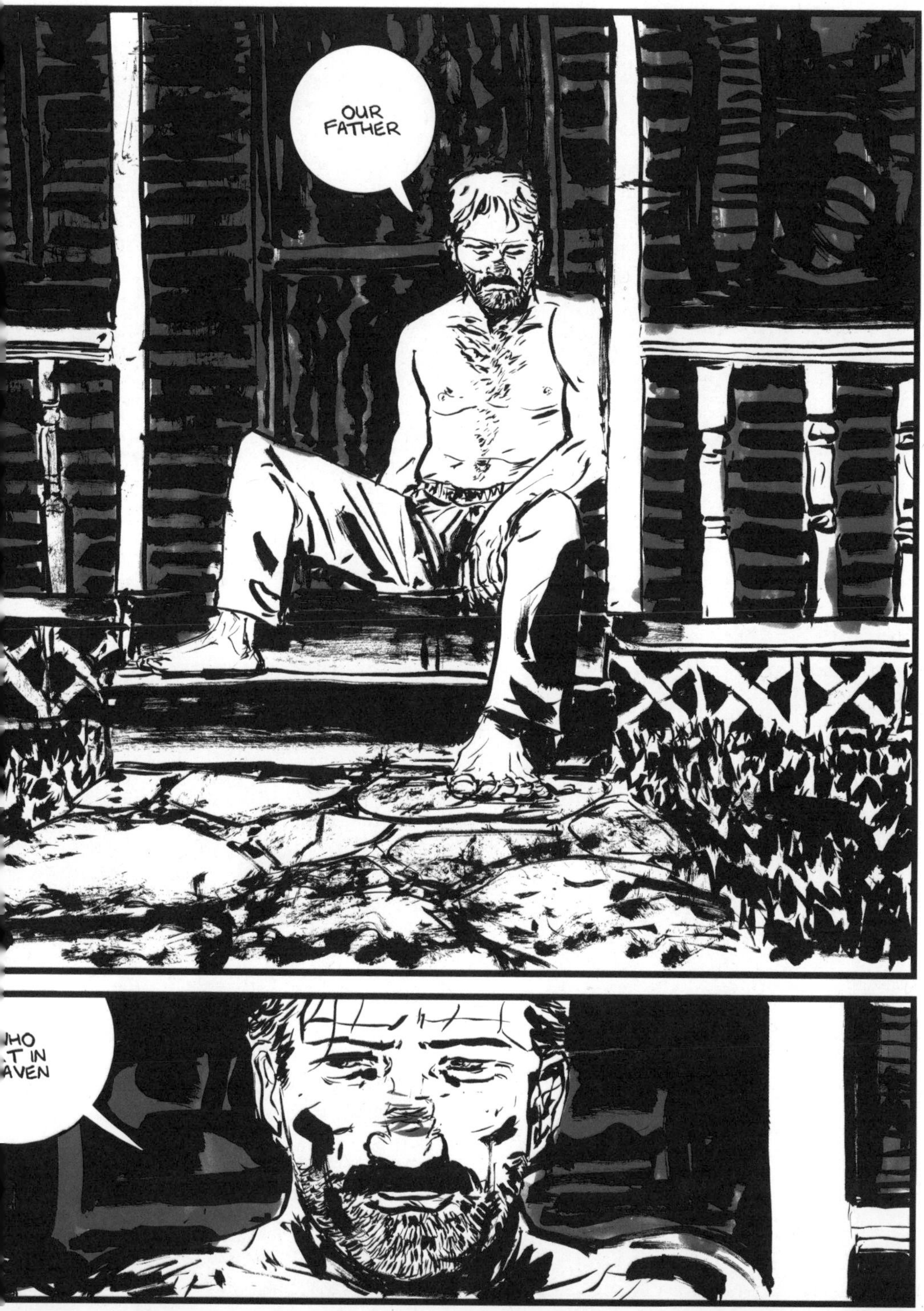
OUR FATHER

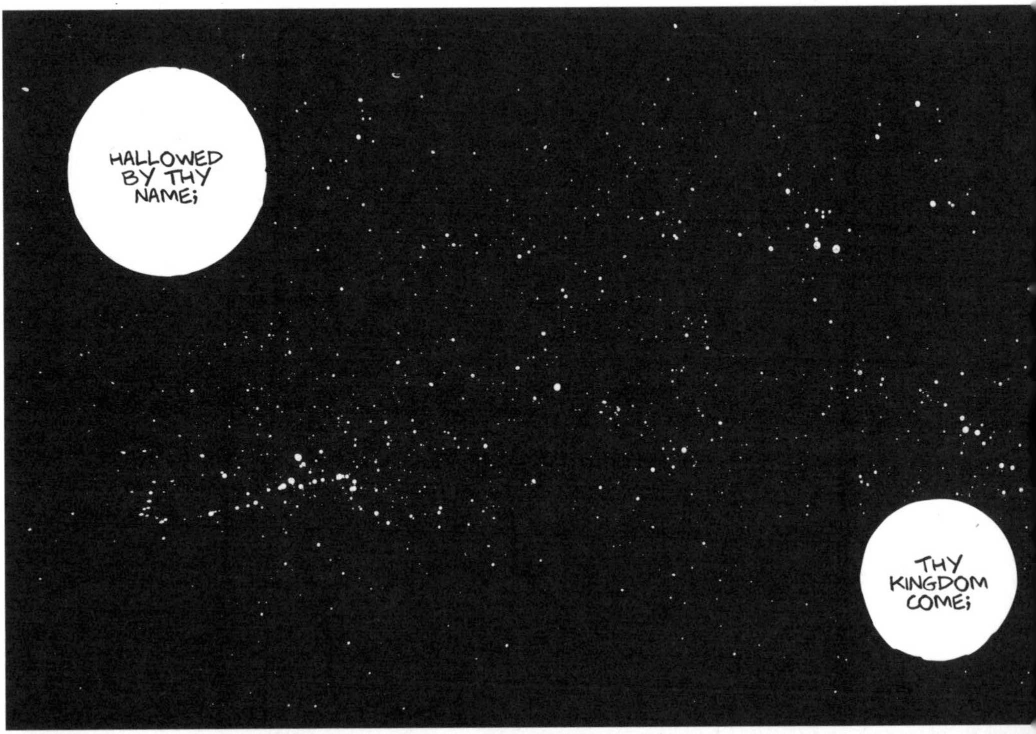
HALLOWED BY THY NAME;
THY KINGDOM COME;

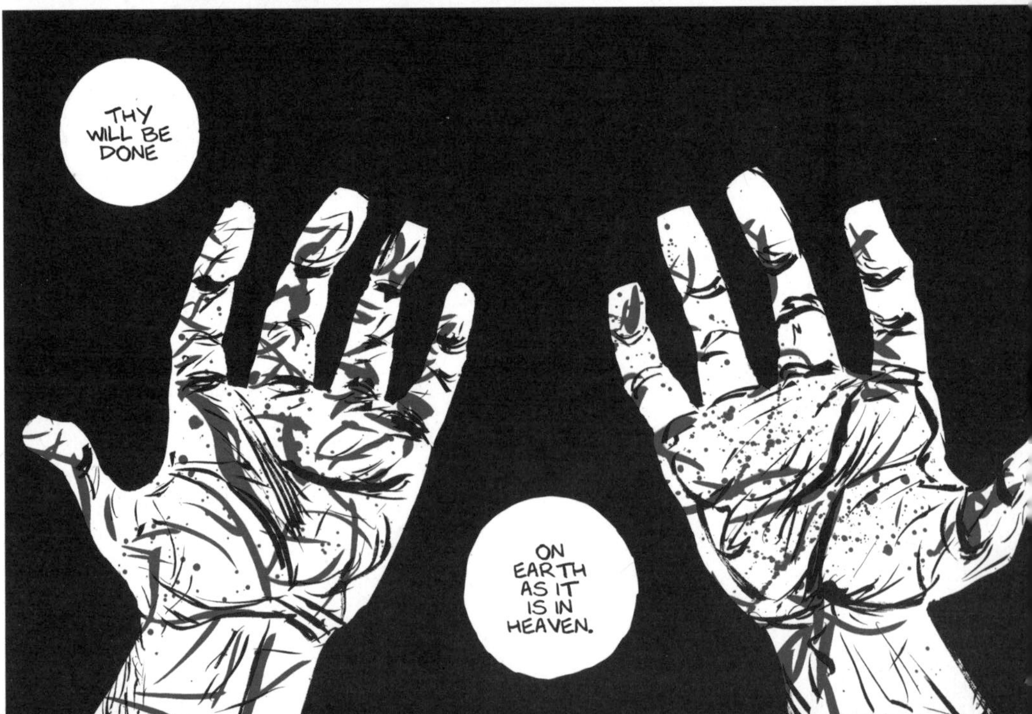
THY WILL BE DONE
ON EARTH AS IT IS IN HEAVEN.

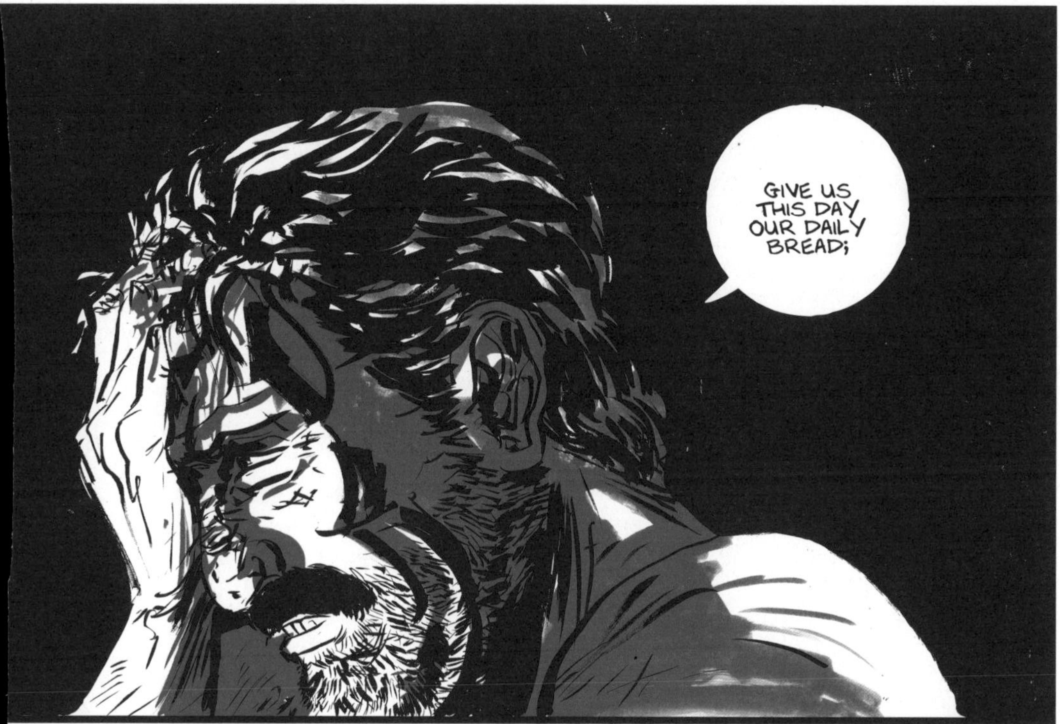
GIVE US THIS DAY OUR DAILY BREAD;

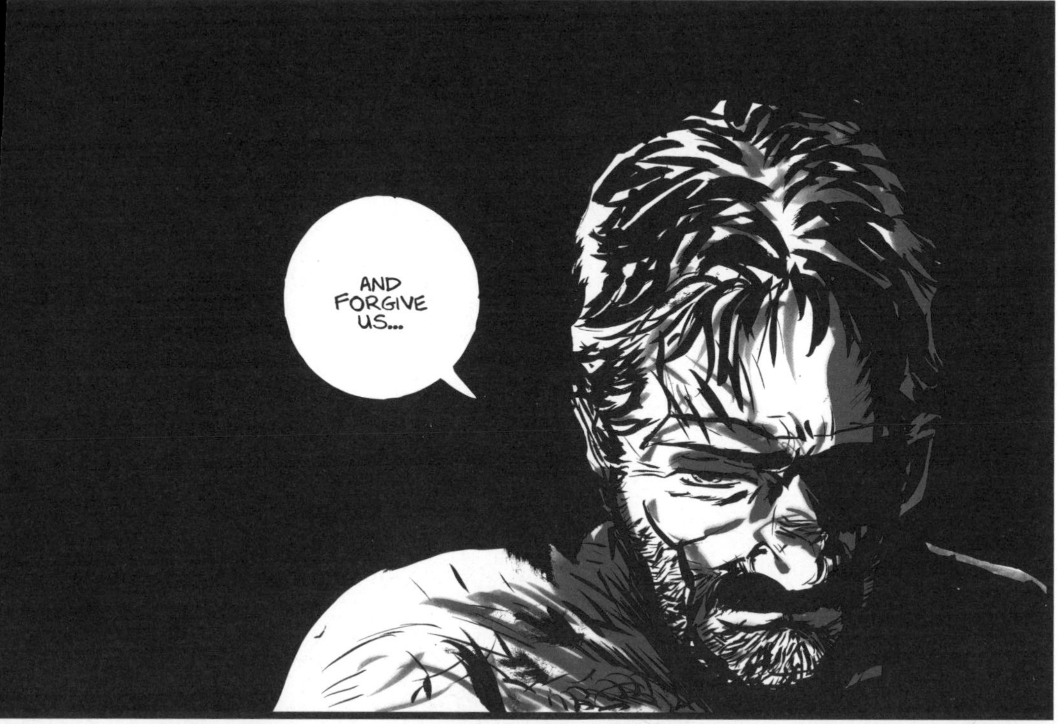
AND FORGIVE US...

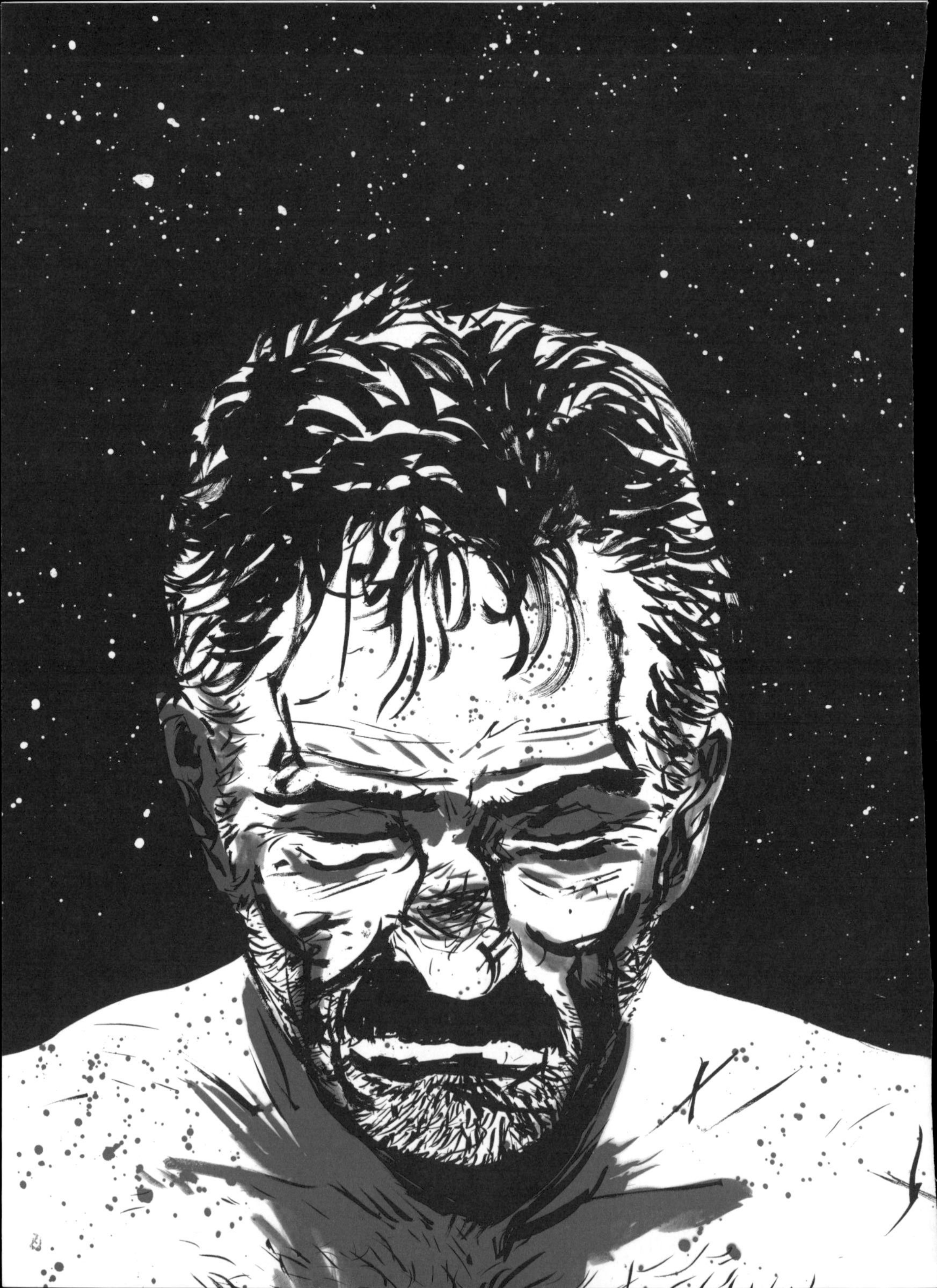

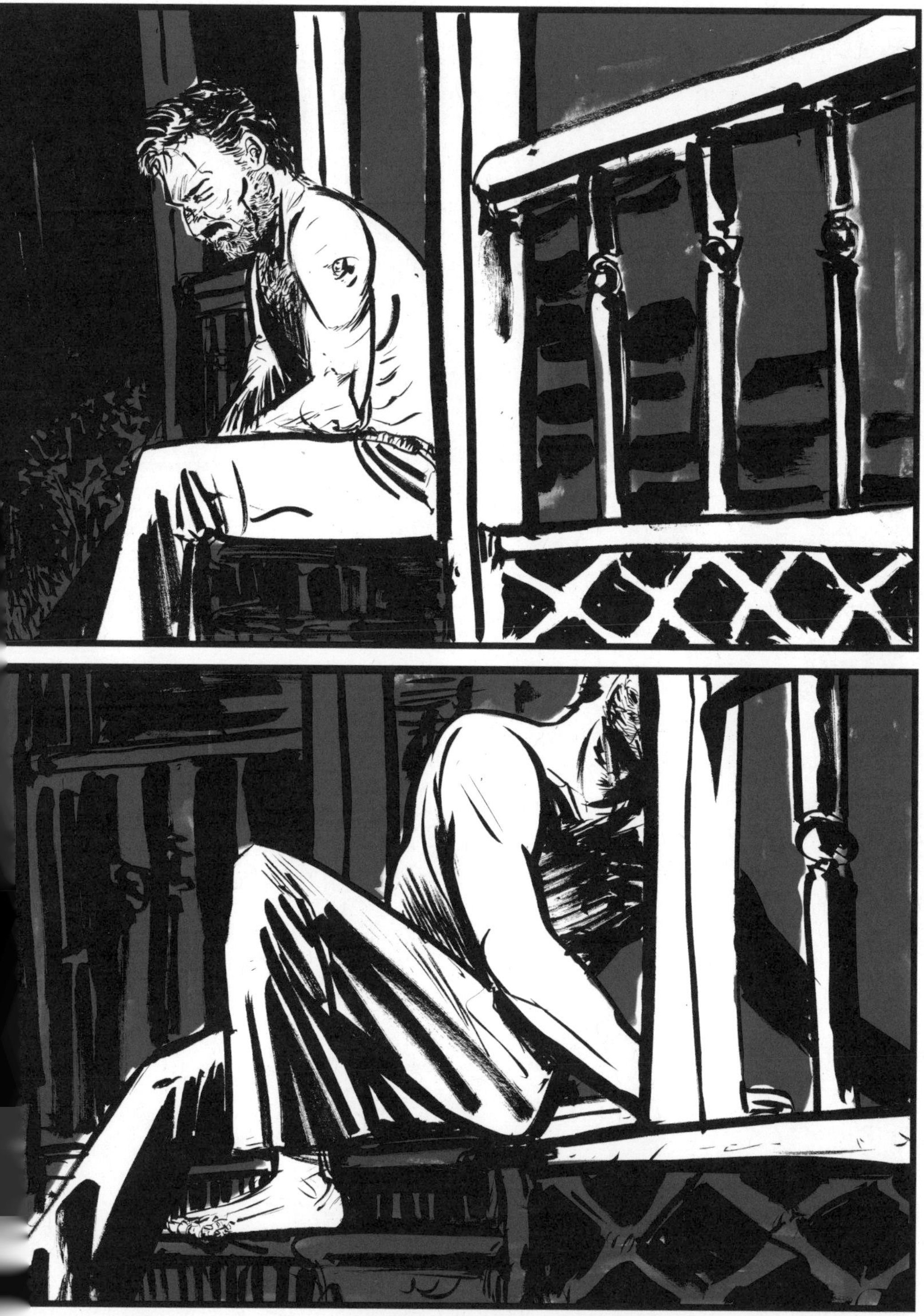

KAFF KAFF

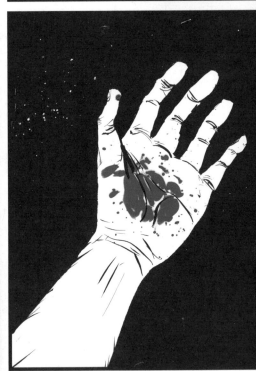

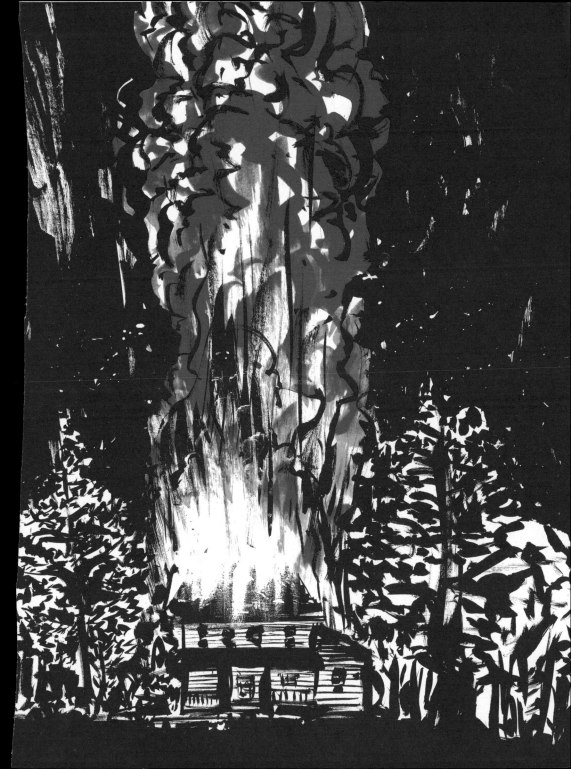

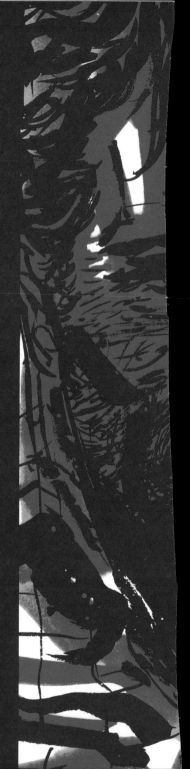

AFTERWORD

BETWEEN THE START OF THIS BOOK AND THE PUBLICATION OF IT, I BECAME A FATHER. I REMEMBER FRANTICALLY TONING, LETTERING, AND CUTTING PATCHES FOR PAGES JUST TRYING TO WRAP IT ALL UP BEFORE SHE WAS BORN.

IT WILL BE A LONG WHILE BEFORE SHE CAN READ THIS BOOK. I HOPE THAT WHEN SHE CAN, IT WILL FEEL MORE LIKE FICTION AND LESS LIKE REALITY, THAT SHE WON'T HAVE A FRAME OF REFERENCE FOR IT, SHE'LL ASK WHAT WAS GOING ON, AND I CAN REMINISCE ABOUT THIS STRANGE DISTANT PIECE OF HISTORY, AND SHE CAN REPLY, "THAT REALLY HAPPENED?"

UNTIL THEN THOUGH, I HOPE THAT HOUSE ON FIRE PROVIDED YOU WITH SOMETHING OF VALUE, AND THAT IT PROVIDES YOU WITH SOME SENSE OF CATHARSIS LIKE IT DID FOR ME WHILE CREATING IT.

- MATT BATTAGLIA, 2023

TIGHTROPE

One of the more obscure pleasures of working with someone on a book is the way you can get to know them and their art skills through the process, the deepest method I know short of actually sitting there with them in the studio while they draw their pages.

I met Matt Battaglia through the Living the Line YouTube page, and in the year that it took for HOUSE ON FIRE to go from a cover sketch and a summary to the finished book you have in your hands, the two of us have had a chance to talk a lot about comics and art. Especially enlightening was picking over some of Matt's favorite books with him, discussing his formative influences as a cartoonist, and gradually using that knowledge to build a deeper picture of him as an artist and writer.

In the three books that Matt, Carson Grubaugh, and I have dissected together, I think you get a good flavor of Matt's interests and the shoulders he stood on while building his own skills. From *Lone Wolf and Cub* artist Goseki Kojima, Matt liberally borrows from the painterly qualities of his surface finish, and his nimble approach to action, as well as attention to mood and environment. From Hugo Pratt of *Corto Maltese* fame, Matt takes both bold brush line and deep abstraction of value, with dense application of black and uncanny combinations of reality and rubbery action. And from Paul Pope, especially his seminal work *100%*, Matt takes the calligraphic approach to mark-making, and the strengths of a near-future setting as a means of abstracting and analyzing personal experiences.

And I don't think it's a secret to say there are personal experiences lurking within this narrative, however fictionalized and transformed. It's most apparent in the passionate delivery that always moves the pages forward, even when the narrative is sometimes obscure.

This is the generosity of narrative that first drew me to Matt's work in the first place. His willingness to allow the space for interpretation, his trust in his audience to take the events of the story and draw their own conclusions.

One more note on the art before I leave you. Matt had an interesting process with these pages, in that, as far as I know, he didn't reference anything directly while working on the book. No photos, no mirrors, nothing but occasionally glancing at the toy truck I practically begged him to buy at the start of the book. The result of this is a liveliness and vitality to the characters that is quite rare in this age of ubiquitous phone cameras and unending Google search results and digital "posing" programs and AI image generation and and and...

The artwork you see here is a simple combination of his line art (the black) and wash (the orange), drawn on an overlay and then digitally composited. In instances where one of us was unhappy with a page or panel, he simply redrew it. As his pencils were essentially only quick roughs, each page ends up being a performance in ink, where his movement across the page is visible to the careful reader who's alert to the process. This gives the whole book, but the action scenes in particular, a tightrope quality that is increasingly rare in a world more and more focused on perfection of performance.

Myself, I'd much rather see the hand wend its way across the page.

– SEAN MICHAEL ROBINSON, 2023

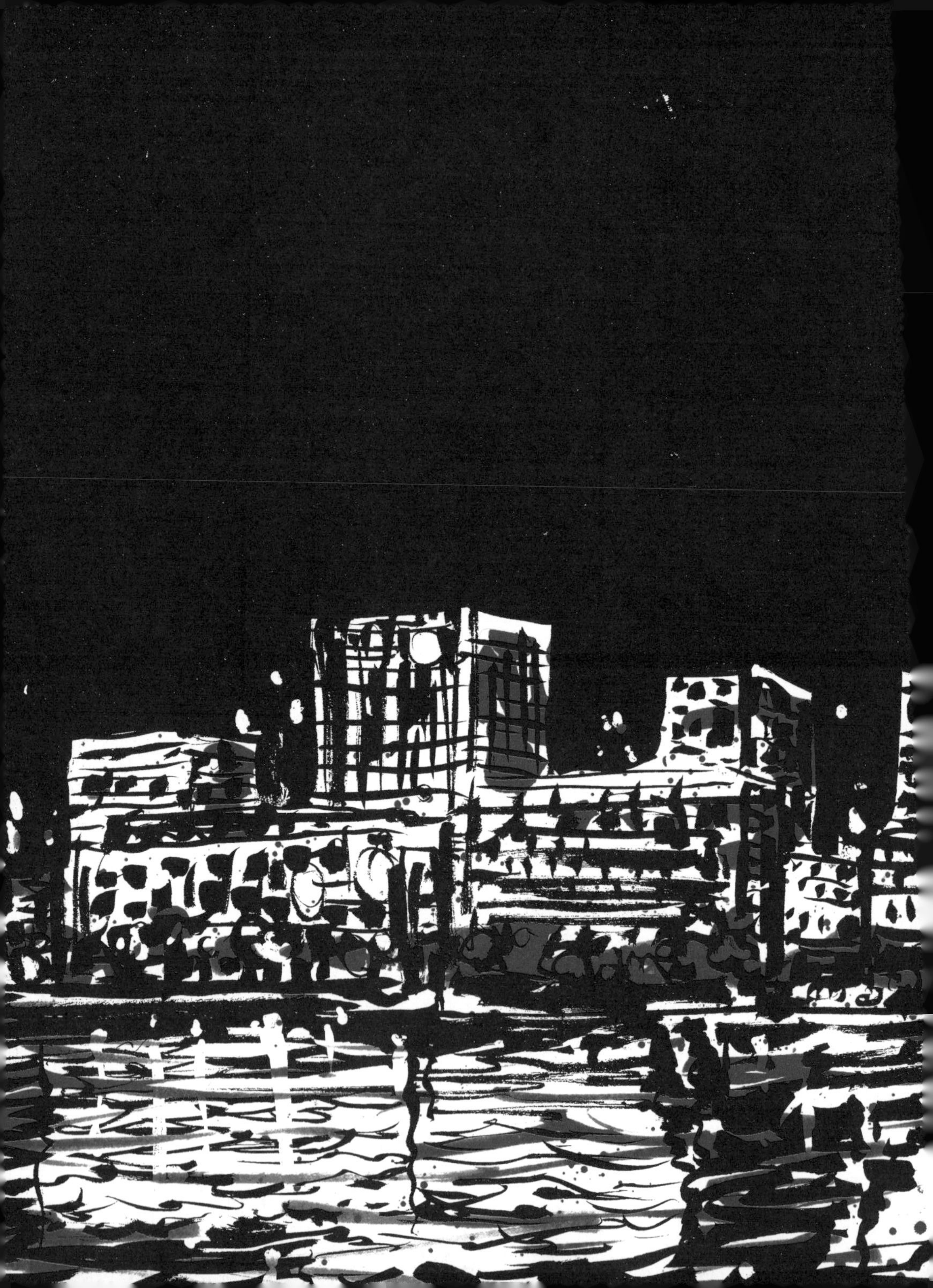